Eugene Doyen has taught scriptwriting for over twenty years, and this book extends his knowledge of imagination and storytelling technique into the work of novel writing.

This book, *Novel Writing: Imagination on the Page* will make it possible for you to identify, understand and develop the skills you need to successfully start and complete a fiction novel.

This book is designed and written to help you succeed: to be creative, to tell stories, and to write the novel you want to write.

Novel Writing
Imagination on the Page

Novel Writing: Imagination on the Page © 2012 Eugene Doyen.
Creative Commons Attribution 2.0
ISBN 978-1-291-11266-5

Contents

The Aim of this Book	7
Knowing what is Creative Writing	9
Developing your Storytelling Skills	17
Defining Yourself as a Writer	37
Storytelling Technique	49
Writing Technique	89
Planning and Writing your Novel	113

The aim of this book

This book will make it possible for you to identify, understand and develop the skills you need to successfully start and complete a fiction novel.

There are three problems that often undermine a first-time author:

- Thinking about writing a novel, but never really starting
- Starting a novel, but never finishing it

And perhaps most dispiriting of all:

- Writing a novel this is just not good enough: it's badly written with weak storytelling

To make sure that you know how to avoid the pitfalls that lead to an unfinished, or poor quality novel, this book helps you understand and assess:

- Your writing skills
- Your creative ability in terms of being able to conceive and develop a long story
- Your storytelling skills: your ability to use narrative and literary techniques
- Your ability to prepare, plan, write and finish your novel

There are six parts to this book and each one deals with specific topics:

Knowing what is creative writing

- How does creative writing differ from other types of writing?
- How can your writing skills be developed?

Developing your storytelling skills

- How can you develop your storytelling skills?
- How can you develop your own stories?

Defining yourself as a writer

- As a storyteller, as a writer, what's your motivation?
- What do you want to write?

Storytelling technique

- Do you have an understanding of narrative terminology that will support you in developing a successful story?
- How will you plan and structure your book?

Writing technique

- How will you define the writing style of your novel?
- What are the stages in writing a novel?

Planning and writing your novel

- What planning can you do to support the writing of your novel?
- What makes a book publishable?

Knowing what is Creative Writing

There is no set formula for creativity or for writing a novel. You can use this book to create your own understanding of yourself as a writer; how your imagination works, what working method suits you. This book sets out a range of questions; answering them will help you define yourself as a writer and support you in becoming a successful author. In essence you are asking:

- What kind of stories do I want to write?
- How will I devise an emotional, involving story?
- What skills do I have as a writer?
- What writing and creative skills do I need to develop?
- How can I plan and write a novel to be sure that it is written to a professional level that is suitable for publishing?

What is creative writing?
Often, when someone mentions 'writing', they envisage this as the actual physical, mechanical process of writing; putting pen to paper or fingers to keyboard. This presumption can in turn lead to the acceptance that the physical activity of actually putting the words on the page defines most of what successful writing requires; practical competence in sentence construction, spelling and punctuation. However, this is a limited definition, and one that is not helpful if you want to define and develop yourself as a creative writer: imaginative writing goes far beyond the creation of sentences with correct spelling and grammar.

It might be best to consider creative writing as having four elements that intertwine and overlap to make a successful writer.

One: **The mechanics of writing**
The knowledge and ability to put words down on the page: simple and complex sentences, clarity of expression, correct use of grammar, spelling and punctuation. These writing skills can be developed through study and practice, and by:

- Writing regularly in a variety of forms: letters, journals, diaries, business writing, academic writing, short stories

Like a musician who practices regularly, the more writing you do the more proficient you become. Professional writers often keep journals or write voluminous amounts of letters. This type of personal, not-intended-for-publication writing is of benefit because non-fiction writing allows you to develop your writing ability, but without the demands of storytelling and style.

To develop your knowledge and competence in the mechanics of writing you can also:

- Improve your writing through the use of guides and reference books

- Improve your writing by understanding the prose technique of specific authors

By studying the very specific construction of sentences, the use of words, the use of punctuation, the grammar and paragraph construction of a particular author, this will provide a very good, very concrete example of the mechanics of writing. This is not the textual interrogation and analysis of literary theory, but a detailed study of technique: how a specific author builds a novel and tells a story; sentence by sentence, paragraph by paragraph.

Two: **Creating stories**

While someone is able to write clear, coherent sentences and well-structured paragraphs, can they imagine and create an interesting, engaging and entertaining story? The skills needed to put stories down on paper does require practical writing ability, but the imagining of them is a different process. This aspect of writing, the imagining of a story, is not dealt with in most writing guides, and it is often overlooked as the essential foundation for creative writing. Creativity, in terms of storytelling ability can be learned; it is not a special talent that only a few can possess.

A creative writer needs story material that they can use to build their own unique stories and they can gather this material through:

- Undertaking research; to actively get material for stories through reading, visiting, and interviewing.

- Storing personal experiences: consciously gathering stories: what is happening in your own life and the lives of those around you.

- Get other people to tell you their stories and store these as material.

- Study stories; understand plots and stories in detail, be able to recount and retell pre-existing stories.

When a writer has got into the habit of gathering story material they can teach themselves to jig-saw. To create complete and complex stories by:

- Using material from different sources to make a single coherent and unique story.

- Elaborating on material they have found, and enhancing it through their own imagination, to increase its dramatic impact and clarity

Three: **Improving storytelling with narrative technique**

There is the story and there is the telling of the story. A story can be told well or it can be told badly. To develop storytelling skills it's necessary to be able to make use of many of the concepts, the terminology that is set out in books and study guides which deal with creative writing. This involves such terms as; conflict, through-lines, beats, plot points, set ups, pay offs, foreshadowing, mirroring, climax, back story, unseen action, misdirection, suspense, disrupting incident. To make use of these terms:

- Become familiar with narrative and storytelling terminology through writing guides and through the study of literary terms.

- Learn to apply literary and storytelling terms to stories that you read and then learn to use these terms when writing your own stories

- Use an understanding of narrative terminology to develop and improve your own stories

If you don't have a grasp of literary and storytelling terminology you have nothing to use to test your story against: judging a story by saying, 'I like the story, or I don't like the story' is not helpful in any practical sense: You need to know if your story is well told, not if you like it or not. Narrative and literary terminology are essential because they give you concepts to help you understand and evaluate what you've written. However, storytelling technique only refines a story; it is imagination that creates the story. An understanding of 'misdirection', or 'suspense', isn't the basis for a story. Terminology only offers techniques for storytelling.

Four: **Planning your writing**

A novel is a long work. It needs stamina to complete a big project. Therefore, it is good to be able to plan your writing so that you can see the task ahead and pace yourself.

If a standard novel is around 80,000 words and you can write 20,000 words a month, to a high standard, then the novel will take four months to write. (With re-writing, editing and polishing, add an extra two months) This is six months for a short novel and it is the pace that a very prolific professional full-time author might achieve. (Not including the time to create and imagine the plot)

For a person working part-time on a novel, then the length of time to finish a complete a first draft increases. If a writer can produce 2,000 words a week, then it is 40 weeks to get to a first draft of 80,000 words, and then six months to re-write, edit and polish. This is a year and a half for a short novel. Longer novels can be 120,000, even 150,000 words, and for a part-time writer the work will extend to two, even three years. (Many literary novelists only produce a book every three or four years)

For a new writer, seeing the scale of the task of writing a novel is important because it allows them to plan realistically and to judge how the work is going. It also tells the writer how much time each week they need to spend writing. If, in a two-hour writing session, a good writer is likely to produce 500 words, it then needs four sessions a week to produce 2,000 words. This is roughly, in total, a day-a-week writing, and possibly too much for a part-time writer.

Planning can also identify what you are doing with your writing time. Correcting and honing each word and sentence as you go during the very first draft is wasteful, if you then have to cut and re-write the novel to control its length, or you decide to significantly change the story after the first draft.

It is efficient to see the process of writing the novel in different stages:

Story Outline: The story as a short synopsis, just one or two pages – around one thousand words. Try to have the entire story, a sense of the characters and a sense of the structure: beginning, complications, development, crisis, climax, and ending.

Story outlines allow you to create a long story, but in a summarized form. You can decide after writing a number of story outlines, which one you think will make a good novel. Novelists, such as Joseph Conrad and Raymond Chandler have developed their short stories into novels. It's a good way to work, and avoids writing a book that falls apart because it ends up as an incomplete story.

Treatment with Chapter Breakdown: The story written in 4,000 to 5,000 words, broken down into a chapter structure. With the plan being that each chapter in the book will be around two thousand words when the book is fully written: so, roughly thirty chapters for a book that will end up being around 60,000 words.

If you can produce a treatment with a chapter breakdown you can understand what events will take place in each chapter and this enables you to think about how you will write and describe this part of the story in 2000 words. The chapter breakdown will also tell you how long it will take to write your novel: 40,000 words – a year to write, 80,000 words - two years, and 120,000 words – four years.

First Draft: Writing to get the story written in full: using the chapter breakdown to structure the book. Not re-writing, correcting or polishing.

You can change the plot and chapter breakdown at this stage, but these sorts of changes will all add to the length of time it will take to finish the novel. It's best, if you can, to write the novel you planned in the chapter breakdown, but if this does need to be changed, then the first draft stage is a far better place to make this decision, much better than when you have entirely finished the first draft, or when you proof-read the book.

Rewriting: Re-working the first draft to sort out the coherence and clarity. Spending time making sure that the story works well, that it has no obvious mistakes. This is period of writing is a good way to improve a first draft. It's also the time that you might want to work with an editor; someone to advise and guide you about how to improve your novel.

Editing: Removing what's unnecessary, repetitive and trimming elements that are overwritten. Cutting the text, editing out sections before final correcting for spelling and punctuation saves time, because you don't perfectly proofread what you will later cut.

Polishing: Adding final refinements to the prose; getting your sentences just right; checking spelling punctuation and grammar.

This is the final stage, not the first stage. Here you have to discipline yourself not to start re-writing and it's the point in the writing of a novel where you might use a proof-reader to ensure that everything is correct in terms of spelling, punctuation and grammar.

There are other documents that a writer will find useful for their novel: Such a character profiles and a style sheet, and these are described later in this book.

Summary: **The four elements of creative writing**

Novel writing, creative writing, consists of four components that are inter-linked:

- Practical writing skills: good sentence and paragraph construction; which can be learned through practice

- Being able to conceive and imagine stories, which is a skill that can be developed over time, through research and by developing your imagination.

- Being able to write and develop stories using storytelling technique – which can be developed by studying literary and narrative terminology

- Being able to successfully plan the writing of a long piece of work, can be done by preparing a story outline, a chapter breakdown and then working through the first draft, editing, re-writing, polishing and proofing.

Assess your writing ability

What stage have you reached in terms of writing skills and storytelling ability? Using your understanding of the four elements involved in creative writing, ask yourself which areas you have mastered.

Writing ability: how often do you write and what do you write? What is your writing history? Is it mainly academic writing, business writing, journals or diaries, correspondence; letters, emails, texts? How much fiction writing have you done? Have you written short stories, novels, parts of novels? You might be a very skillful writer in one area of writing, such as business writing, and this will feed into your ability as a creative writer, but four areas of skills are needed in order to be a successful storyteller in terms of novel writing.

Storytelling ability: Are you a creator of stories? A novel is a long complex story. Even if the events are small scale they have to be well conceived and well told. Do you tell stories to your friends? What sort of stories have you created? Does your storytelling ability extend into plays, novels and other types of stories?

Telling anecdotes and having a broad idea for a story is a skill that many possess. The long story, the play, the novel, needs a level of complexity and sophistication that requires work. If you're a new writer, why not write short stories and when you're ready develop one particular story into a full novel. You can experiment and try out ideas in the short form before committing to the time and work needed for a full novel.

Understanding of storytelling technique: Do you have a working knowledge of storytelling vocabulary? Do you have a range of terms and ideas that allows you to test and consider stories?

Any specialist will be able to use the vocabulary, the terminology which relates to their area of work. How many terms can you list that you can use to help you with your storytelling? Writing a novel needs a clear grasp of storytelling technique; something to guide your writing.

Planning and writing a long project: What's the longest project you've written? Have you written a thesis? Do you write regularly? What's your average word count for a writing session? How long will it take you to write a thousand words to a standard that is good enough for publishing?

It's fine to be a slow writer and, it's fine to write quickly, but to plan a novel and to be able to consider your progress you need a sense of how long it will take you to finish: four months, a year, two years, four years, ten years.

You can just start a novel, not knowing where it's going, but this can lead to disaster; a confused over-written book with no coherent style. Planning, by writing an outline and a chapter breakdown is a good idea, even if you drop this method later. A complex work, a novel of any size, is supported by a good plan.

Planning gives you time to think about the story and to structure the narrative and dramatic elements of the plot without having to worry about writing good prose, or the use of language and the writing style of your novel.

Developing Your Storytelling Skills

Creating Stories through Jig-Sawing

Imagine that you are making a picture puzzle, a jig-saw. You start with a single, barely recognizable element, and you begin to build from there.

After a while, when you survey the pieces of the picture that you have put together, you can see the, initial, separate parts of the image, slowly forming into a whole. You can see distinct parts that look like they are going to join up, but they're not exactly the right: something is missing. There are also pieces that seem like they will be part of the picture, eventually, but you have no idea where they should go right now. Overall, you have all the elements; some parts are complete, and there are some large, worrying gaps, but there are also some interesting little pieces that don't seem to go anywhere. However, by slowly surveying, comparing, testing, and working, you find the matching parts and the whole picture is gradually and finally finished.

This jig-saw method is how to describe the creative process of imagining a story. It can happen just in the mind, it could be a story that's told and re-told by the author while working out the details, and for a long work, for, a novel, a script or a play, it is a process that is likely to be worked out on paper, gestated in the mind and the work goes back and forth; thinking and writing a plan, thinking and revising, re-writing and re-planning. Making a story happens through trial and error: inspiration and obstacle, solution and problem.

While the idea of the creative process being a jig-saw may seem to be simply an analogy, I would suggest you treat it as a real and practical solution to the development of storytelling skills. Ideas are fragments; something appeals, something connects and a character or a plot starts to form. At the start, a story is missing a lot of elements, but if you continue to search for them you will eventually find them. Stories don't simply appear finished and complete in the mind and if you simply wait for the whole story to appear you are unlikely to ever start writing or to put down more than a few meager notes. A fragment of an idea may seem like a whole story because it inspires you, it feels like a complete idea, but if you don't work on it, think it through, put in the time and effort to develop it, then your story idea is just a notion; it will remain only a morsel of a whole story.

Something that's true of any type of skill is that the more effort and the more time you put into creating stories the better you will get and the easier the process will become.

In terms of storytelling and creative writing, using the simple idea of the jig-saw technique as the key to understanding the creative process may seem weak; you might try it once or twice and find that it doesn't give you anything substantial. However, if you try it and try it again, and keep working at it, then this method of thinking will start to bear fruit. If you want to learn to drive a car or play a musical instrument you don't give up because it's awkward and difficult to begin with. You need the same approach to creating stories. Early efforts will be patchy. Things will be clichéd. Ends will be missing. You might tell an entire story but no one who hears the story told, or reads it, seems impressed - no one gets it. In this case there is a gap between the compelling, involving story that you think you're telling and how it's understood. Then you learn by creating another new, even better story.

To improve your storytelling you learn how to make sure that there are enough elements in the plot so that stories don't collapse. You understand how to clearly establish characters so that personalities and relationships are clear. You start to understand what will build interest and excitement, you learn to prune and cut what is unnecessary or confusing. Finally, as you develop your storytelling skills you become more adept. The piecing together of fragments becomes quicker, clearer. You don't have so many failures. You can make a specific focused effort and produce an idea to solve a specific plot or character problem. Finally, you have learnt how to create stories.

Using this simple idea, the jig-saw technique, will work if you give it the time and effort to develop. Also, there are ways to start using this method that can make your progress as a storyteller far easier than others.

Jig-saw technique: fiction from fact

If you're going to create a story using the jig-saw technique you need material: ideas, events, people, places, moments; elements that you can piece together. You can rely on your own experience, you certainly will use your own experiences, but it is far easier to start from a clearer and more certain foundation; a story that already exists.

So many stories are based on factual events, either famous or little known. In the novels written by Robert Harris historical fact is used to develop original fiction:

> **Fatherland:** A murder mystery set in Germany as though the Nazi's had won the second-world war.

Archangel: A plot generated out of the Soviet, Cold War, era and based on the idea of Stalin's legacy

The Ghost: A murder mystery surrounding a British Prime Minister accused of allowing prisoners to be taken from Britain for torture. A story using accusations made of the British Government, during the time of Tony Blair.

Engima: A story of intrigue, surrounding the World War II enigma decoding machine

Lustrum: A dramatization of Caesar and other prominent Roman figures.

By using pre-existing historical events and people Robert Harris has the material, a setting and characters, in which it is possible to imagine a fictional story.

Rather than waiting for inspiration working on a story from fact is a great support. History, or news, or documentary, gives the writer a story world, past events, a range of characters, and a storyteller can pick and choose, and create making their own fictional version or alternative – a new story. Once the work on the plotting for the book begins, if there is a blank in the imagination, it's possible to fill in any gaps in a story by doing research; the writer reads up on their subject and finds related material.

With this approach the writer uses their jig-sawing skills to shape and prune their story until it's shaped it into a well-structured and engaging plot and while this can still require a lot of work, it is better than starting from a blank page.

To work from fact you do not necessarily need to use famous people, and your sources can be TV, Books, newspapers and magazines. For example the feature film *The Fast and The Furious* was developed from a magazine story. To get to grips with creating fiction from fact, and if you wanted to try your hand at writing short stories, rather than a full-length novels to develop your storytelling skills, then you might look for short factual events; incidents, short episodes.

A foundation in character

Dashiell Hammett and other writers such as Raymond Chandler, Colin Dexter, and Carl Hiaasen base their stories on a character that the author uses again and again. This approach is probably the most certain way to have a successful writing career that can span both books and films.

While all the characters in a book will have some relationship to their author one often gets a sense that the fictional hero or heroine of the tale is an idealized alter ego of the author. Certainly, the Op and Sam Spade stem from the experiences and viewpoint of Dashiell Hammett, (both author and fictional characters were private investigators) while the characters of the fictional forensic pathologists Kay Scarpetta and Tempe Brennan relate in turn to the career and knowledge of Patricia Cornwall (who worked for several years in the world of forensic pathology) and Kathy Reichs who is herself a forensic pathologist.

The link between fictional character and author does not have to be as close in terms of professional life as is the case with Hammett, Cornwall and Brennan. Colin Dexter who worked for the Oxford Examination Board had no experience as a detective, but he created Detective Inspector Morse. However, like Morse, Colin Dexter is university educated, is intellectual in his pursuits, is rigorous in his use of English, and lives in the environs of Oxford, so it is easy to see how Dexter's own life provides a setting and personality for his fictional character. But of course Dexter was never a police officer and has never investigated a murder; unlike Inspector Morse.

While a fictional character may be created primarily in the mind, as an extension of the author's personality, you can still use fact to support a fictional character. In the Sharpe novels written by Bernard Cornwell, his hero, Richard Sharpe, fights in Portugal as a soldier in The Duke of Wellington's army in the early 1800's and the setting for these stories follows the campaign of the Peninsula War.

In *Sharpe's Havoc*, the eponymous hero fights at Oporto, in Portugal, in May 1809 and the action and geography of the fictional story closely follows that of the historic battle. In the actual fighting the French drove the Portuguese and British across the river and this is what happens in Sharpe's Havoc. At the end of the novel, Sharpe and his men set up their defenses in a Catholic seminary, and this building, its shape and position can be seen in the maps of Oporto used at the time of Wellington. The skill with this kind of fact-into-fiction storytelling is to meld the fictional Sharpe into the historic events and to give him a task that will create a specific and significant story for his character.

Bernard Cornwell has also used this approach to write a trilogy of books based on the legends of King Arthur. From both the Sharpe novels and the King Arthur trilogy one can see how fictional characters can take on historical roles and the fictional historical novel is of course a recognized genre with books such as *The English Patient* and *Cold Mountain* using this type of authentic historical setting for their stories.

Another approach to mixing fictional characters with other sources when creating stories is used by Anthony Horowitz. He has created a fictional spy, Alex Rider, who inhabits a world very similar to the fictional world of James Bond.

Alex Rider is a boy of only 14, but works for MI5. In both series of books, James Bond and Alex Rider, there are secret agents who use specialized secret gadgets, who get involved in dangerous chases, and defeat arch-villains who want world domination. This means that with Alex Rider, a new fictional character has been created, but he exists in a fictional environment created primarily by another author, Ian Fleming.

While this approach to storytelling, re-working setting and characters, is very specific in terms of the similarity between Alex Rider and James Bond, this is often used more broadly when authors write using the genres of fantasy or sci-fi, where the type of worlds created by established authors have many features which are used by new writers.

The fantasy world of the Harry Potter books has some overlaps with the world of *Lord of The Rings*, where the mystical and magical creatures in these stories have similar powers and characteristics. There is the evil Lord Sauron in *Lord of the Rings* and the evil Lord Voldermort in Harry Potter, and in both a young hero is tasked as part of his destiny to be the one who destroys the evil Lord. In fact with any forms of genre writing, vampire, crime, SF, Fantasy, the author is using a pre-established set of conventions for character, plot and setting. New authors often feel that genre writing is less original and therefore less good, but writing a story in a setting that attracts and satisfies is in fact often what keeps an author going, and supports them in creating their own original stories.

A foundation in environment

An author can rely on a single character as the focus for their writing, or work from a range of characters that inhabit a similar environment. The author Edith Wharton writes about American high society, the society she lived in, and she uses both male and female characters to carry her own personality and ideas. Scott Fitzgerald wrote about the Jazz Age, nineteen-twenties America, where his own relationship with his wife is displaced into several of his novels using a range of characters. Once again the key to working in fiction is to start from a clear situation and build upon this foundation rather than trying to create an entirely new world

Problem solving

One way to generate a story from actual places and situations is problem solving. If you wanted to rob a casino, how would you go about it? In this case you would create the story by planning the crime.

The novel, *The Eagle Has Landed,* was developed by Jack Higgins, from the pre-existing idea where there was a plan during World War Two to capture Winston Churchill; just as Mussolini had been rescued by German paratroopers from Italy. Setting himself this creative storytelling problem (How would it be possible to assassinate Churchill) Higgins found a location for it to happen and created characters to carry out and thwart this endeavor. The same approach has been used in various stories; robbing the Crown Jewels in *The Jokers* and a casino in *Ocean's Eleven*. This problem-solving idea can be used on almost any scheme you want to choose and the difference between this approach and an idea based solely in the imagination is that one can research how the Crown Jewels and casinos are protected, so that it's possible to plan a crime and generate the story through research.

Semi-autobiography, roman à clef

Fiction can also be very close to real life with the actual events compressed and re-ordered for fiction and the names of the characters chosen to conceal the person. Writers who have used this method are Charles Bukowski, John Fante, Henry Miller, Silvia Plath and Jack Kerouac. In this kind of writing the skill is to recognize what will make an interesting story from the events of your own life and how to structure them into a story for drama or prose.

Originality

Given that successful professional writers are developing their stories using other lives, their own lives and they develop ideas from other fictions it becomes hard to find any piece of work that could be defined as completely singular or original in its conception. Working from this understanding, the job of an author is to create stories through gathering, choosing, ordering and structuring rather than from the far more ephemeral and mysterious thing that creativity and originality is supposed to be. A writer is like a cook gathering ingredients, putting them together, seeing what elements they like and what appeals to them and this is why the idea of jig-sawing and learning how to jig-saw is the key to imagination and storytelling.

Getting started: developing an original story

There is the first jolt of an idea that *might* create a story. It could come from:

- A personal event: something that happened to you, to someone you know, or it can be a story that you've heard

- It might come from a theme. Such as; will people take personal responsibility for others in a crisis? What will a patriot do for their country?

- It could come from a factual source: book, television, news, internet

- It could be from a fictional source: film, play or book. You will add new elements. You could have an idea that tries to improve or oppose an existing story

- Your story could be within a genre that you particularly like or understand very well.

An idea will not develop into a full story unless it has some resonance with you. Success in storytelling will come from recognizing and focusing on ideas that you like and which you can write in a format, within a genre, with a dramatic structure that connects with reader. To develop an idea into a story you need:

- A plot that is coherent and works within a credible world

- Characters with back stories, with motivations, with conflicts and relationships

- A narrative structure that tells the story within a dramatic and involving format

Things to do to develop stories

Note ideas, sit with them, think about them, work on them; build an idea into a story with events and things happening: a static story is no good.

Interrogate your ideas: are they any good? Is your idea developing? Is the jolt of an initial idea coming to nothing? Is it time to move on to another idea?

- Outline your story, then put that outline into a plan that identifies the separate chapters for a book: is it a whole story? Is it enough for a novel? Is it too complex and confusing?

- Read your story aloud. Read it to someone else. Do they 'get it'? Do they enjoy it? If you're the only person who understands the story, then you've probably got a problem with your characters and motivation.

- Stand back and judge your story. Finish a story and after a few weeks read it again. With this gap in time, you will see what it is that's missing or fails in the story, because it's not well told. What's weak will come through, and also what's good will be clear and certain. This practice, coming back to the writing after a period of time, works well to judge a book, because you're reading the story from a distance, and you can see it from the standpoint of a reader, rather than a writer.

Start a story using a source

The concept of jig-sawing is one that sets out how to develop stories by moving narrative elements around and fitting them together to make a coherent story. These narrative elements come from a range of sources and while there is no absolutely clear way to find a start for a good story idea it's useful to know where to look and also to note, that more of than not, in creating stories, writers' use a range of sources for a single work.

Using established formats and genres

Why start from the blank page? Why start from scratch and reinvent the wheel? Why not look carefully at how established formats and genres tell stories? Choose whatever type of story that appeals to you; thriller, mystery, romance, study it well, and then use it as a springboard. What you add to a format – the setting, the characters, the specifics of the plot are what make the story original.

The problematic aspect of using established formats and genres as your guide is superficiality; where a weak understanding of story genre leads to poor imitations of successful work, and a reliance on what is worn out; the clichés of plotting, using hammy out-of-date stereotypes. Working from a base, a genre, that is established, is a strength, but the writer must avoid re-hashing, and producing hackneyed work.

Developing new work from other stories
If you know a fiction story very well, the precise details of its plot and characters, you can develop a sense of how those characters might behave in another situation and in doing so create a new and different story for them. Can you imagine a sequel? Here you are saying; 'I know this story, but where does it go from here?'

When you watch a film or read a book do you sometimes say; 'The plot didn't work and this is what should have happened ...' If ever you do have those thoughts, then at that moment you have started to create a new and different story.

Though it is not highly publicized the practice of having multiple writers working with the same characters is common; many authors have written Sherlock Holmes and also James Bond stories. This re-use of characters happens in books, television shows, film sequels and film prequels: so, to create your own story why not do this?

Writing for the market
Why not write stories that people want? Look at the top films and the bestseller lists for books. Look at the work of the most successful screenwriters and authors. Can you find a similar type of story, with the same type of characters? Writing for the market can give you a place to start and you can develop your own story style from there. This approach should not be just a case of imitating and copying, but one of developing, changing, and revitalizing.

Working from people
By deciding to devise a story with a person you know or a historical figure, you have already put in place someone, a figure, who you can develop into a story character. This person will give you incidents, relationships, social context and history.

The challenge with real people and real lives is that they do not behave with the consistency of fictional characters and their stories do not necessarily fit into a dramatic structure with a clear set of acts and a suitably powerful and poignant climax. If you work from a person you can't just put them into fiction, you need to make an effort to define them as fictional characters; create a back story for them, give them clear motivations.

Working from true life and history
Putting a story in a historical context gives you a rich environment to work from. You know how the society is structured, what its mores and morals are, what creates conflict in that society and what stories might emerge from this. You can choose a society you know well personally, or one that you have studied during your education or you can research a society that is new to you. A great bonus is that you can find historical sources, visit sites, even, interview participants in the actual events to develop your story idea. You can then create fictional characters who will successfully inhabit that era.

Working from personal events and biography
The closest source of events that might be developed into a story is your personal life. This has good potential but as with other real life sources it needs to be fictionalized and developed. What is interesting and worthwhile as a personal experience is not necessarily of interest to others; a fiction based on a true story still needs to have themes, structure, narrative drive, entertainment. Often, personal stories tend to be incidents, anecdotes, and these bits and pieces don't have the plotting to keep a reader interested. The personal story might fill a couple of pages, but at two hundred pages might well be only a set of episodes.

Jack Kerouac's *On the Road*, is an example where real life characters have been renamed for a fiction novel. This book does have a meandering sense of story, which is the problem for many weak books, but in this case it is saved by having a strong relationship between the two central characters, and by the quality and style of the prose.

It's fine to write a memoir, or a roman à clef, but this is not likely to be something that others want to read, unless the people involved are already famous. The difficulty is that those who regularly read novels are familiar with the genres, the kind of story they like, the type of literature they prefer, and a one-off story, by an unknown writer, has far less appeal to publishers and to the reading public.

Working from places and locations
The specifics of a place, from a country, to a town, to a single building can help you create stories. Specific locations, the shape of rooms, how buildings are laid out, can give you a sense of the possibilities for how action and events can take place. Rather than imagining from scratch what the setting for a story is like it can be much easier to consider an actual place and use this, because then the setting is much more concrete, and it is easier to develop fictional ideas, which are well

thought out. You can always create your own buildings and locations, and even draw maps or diagrams. A story is easier to imagine if you have a plan of the world where the events takes place.

In Robert Harris's novel *Fatherland*, there is a fictional Berlin, and to make sure that the reader understands this there is a map of the city at the start of the book. Similarly, Tolkein, drew maps of his fantasy world of hobbits, elves and orcs. A writer with no clear idea of their fictional world risks being inconsistent and unconvincing when describing action and events in their story.

Working from themes

If you identify a theme or a topic that you want to write a story about you can try to fit it into a range of formats: this theme might be driven by a political viewpoint, a social perspective, a personal belief, or a social issue that occupies or interests you. Rather than just looking for stories almost at random, it is easier to have a theme that creates an environment where a story can grow. If your interest was the effects of slavery, you might not want to write a historical novel, but could shift this situation into another setting.

Working from research

Research can feed into any writing project. But it can also be a source for ideas. If you study a topic, any subject, you can approach it with the idea that you will try and see if stories emerge from this research.

Summary: What to work for to become a creative writer

Gather story material

To ensure that you have enough material at hand to help your storytelling you need to make a commitment to be a storyteller, which means that you will consciously look for and gather story material.

Recognizing your motivation to write

Liking films or books is not enough to want to write. If you can recognize your strongest motivation this can drive you forward and keep you going as a storyteller, rather than you remaining a consumer of stories.

Recognizing your strengths

Just because you like a particular type of story, doesn't mean that you should write it. Your own strengths in storytelling can be quite different from your taste as a consumer. If you find it easier to imagine and write one type of story, then this is probably the right genre for you. Also, you don't have to write for yourself. You could, for instance write for young readers or write stories set in different environments to the world you inhabit.

Putting aside weak or unrealized ideas

Just because you have an idea for a story does not make this a good idea. When you first start thinking about stories any plotting or characters you have may seem precious. These ideas may develop, but don't hang onto a setting or incident that doesn't keep growing. If, after a couple of months, what you're thinking about hasn't built into a structured plot with developed characters, set these bits and pieces of story aside, and begin thinking about another novel. There's no need to completely discard your first ideas, but it's just not giving you enough to start writing. You need to start again.

Give time and effort to developing stories

You have an idea, it's vague, but you have to spend specific time and effort thinking about a full and complete story, working on ideas, mapping it out, re-starting. You can't wait for a story to form fully fledged. The starting idea for a story will die on you if you don't work to develop it.

Keeping notes of story ideas

Days go by in a distracting rush. The habit of making notes, of keeping a store of ideas is important. Good ideas will be lost and vague ideas will never crystallize if you don't put something down on paper, or on computer, and then return to work with these notes.

Keeping successful work habits

You need time to think about your stories and you need time to write. When you commit to a long story you need a lot of time, and a sustained effort and concentration to carry it through.

An original story from Arthur Conan Doyle's *Thor Bridge*

By comparing the Sherlock Holmes short story, *The Problem of Thor Bridge*, and an outline for the plot of a novel, *Brotherly Love*, which is set out below, it's possible to see an example of the re-working and rearranging of pre-existing material to create a new and original story.

If you want to read the text of *The Problem of Thor Bridge* in full it can be found on the web by doing a quick search.

Plotting: *Thor Bridge*
This is the plot of the original story by Arthur Conan Doyle:

Sherlock Holmes is called upon to solve the murder of a rich industrialist's wife. The governess of the house has been convicted of the crime, because she had a meeting arranged with the murdered wife at *Thor Bridge* and no one else was in the vicinity at the time of the killing. Also, a gun matching that used to murder the wife was found in the governess's clothes cupboard.

The solution to the crime is that the wife framed the governess by committing suicide in a way that left the wife lying dead from a bullet wound, but there was no gun in sight. This was achieved by the wife taking a matching pair of guns from her husband, hiding one in the governess's cupboard, then at Thor Bridge attaching the second gun, with string to a weight thrown over the bridge. When the wife shot herself the gun was pulled away and out of sight into the waters of the lake; leaving the governess as the last person to see the wife alive and in possession of a hidden gun.

The outline for the novel *Brotherly Love* makes use of the following features of the first story:

- A person hates someone close to them so much that they are determined to frame them for murder. (In this case a young man, Sebastian, hates his brother, Christopher.)

- A plan is put in place so that a person can kill themselves, and it will look like they have been murdered by another person. This is achieved by having the weapon attached to a length of string so that it will appear not to have been in the possession of, and in the control of, the dead person.

The short story, *Brotherly Love*, based on *The Problem of Thor Bridge* can be read as an example of imaginative thinking, and also as the outline for a novel.

Brotherly Love
Sebastian was, and always would be, three years younger than his brother, Christopher. Perhaps that was the essential problem.

When Sebastian and Christopher's parents divorced, Sebastian stayed with his mother, because he was younger, and Christopher went to live with his father, because he was older.

Sebastian thought that Chris should have stayed with him and with their mother, because they were brothers, and because their father was a betrayer, but Chris didn't seem to care. Chris enjoyed living with his dad.

Then, when Sebastian and Chris were old enough; Chris had just graduated and started working, and Sebastian had enrolled at University, their father bought the brothers a house in London; for the two boys to live in and to share together. Their father could afford to do this, because he was a successful architect who had his own practice.

It would be just the brothers living together – their house

Since Chris was working during the day Sebastian agreed to supervise the moving in and all the deliveries.

The two men who brought the new cooker were pretty annoyed when Sebastian insisted that he wanted it left at the top of the stairs. But, as he explained, with some irritation, he and his brother were going to convert the house into two flats, and then live separately, so he needed the cooker carried up to the first floor.

Sebastian didn't offer the two deliverymen a tip for their extra work; he just told them he wouldn't sign for the cooker unless they put it where he wanted it.

When the cooker stood in place at the top of the stairs Sebastian waited in hiding until Chris came home.

Hiding out of sight on the landing Sebastian heard the front door slam and his brother come into the hallway.

'I'm up here!' Sebastian called out loudly.

'Hi,' Chris answered, as he moved quickly up the first couple of steps of the stairs before he stopped at the sight of the big rectangular box leaning over the top step.

The cooker was still in its brown cardboard packaging.

'What this?' Chris said.

Sebastian popped into view; 'I'm just trying to carry this downstairs. Will you help me with it?'

Chris didn't move. 'What's in the box?'

'Just a cooker.' Sebastian said as he heaved the cooker forward with both hands.

'Jesus Christ!' Chris blurted out as the box tipped towards him.

The cooker didn't spring from its perch and roll from the top step like a deadly boulder as Sebastian hoped; it toppled slowly and heavily forward and Chris was able to jump down into the hallway before he suffered any injury.

Sadly, the cooker didn't even make it all the way down the stairs. After the first bounce, it pivoted on a corner, twisting into the banister, where it broke a few struts before stopping dead.

Chris was the first to speak. 'You idiot - What did you do!'

While they were moving the cooker off the stairs Sebastian explained that the two delivery men had insisted on carrying the box up to the first floor, because that's what the instructions for installation said in their delivery note. Sebastian tried to make this story sound convincing, but it was a lame excuse for what had happened on the stairs and Chris was still angry with him.

The idea for powdered glass came when Sebastian noticed that in the mornings, before his older brother Chris rushed off to work, he always gobbled down a bowl of cereal with plenty of sugar on top.

Sebastian spent the day breaking a bottle, breaking it again, breaking it some more and then crushing it and crushing it until he had turned the bottle into fine ground glass.

Chris spat out his cereal on the first mouthful. 'It's got grit in it.' He announced angrily.

Sebastian offered to take the sugar back to the supermarket to complain about the problem.

Sebastian's next plan would make it appear that Chris had been killed while chasing off a burglar in the middle of the night.

The Victorian terraced house that the two brothers had moved into was on the outskirts of London. It had a long thin back garden that butted onto the Metropolitan tube line. There was a gap in the fence that led directly to the track.

During the purchase, when the house had been surveyed there had been a tree that the surveyor noted had grown tall enough to obstruct and endanger a train if it ever fell, so it had to be removed.

As part of the purchase agreement the previous house owners had agreed to get the tree cut down, but the work had also demolished a section of the garden wall, because the tree was so close to it, and the tree's roots ran under the wall's foundations. At the moment solicitors' letters were being exchanged between Sebastian's father and the previous owners over who should pay the money to make good the damage to the brickwork.

Sebastian began banging on Chris's bedroom door in the middle of the night.

'Chris, wake up!' Sebastian urged, 'You have to get up there's someone outside.'

'What are you talking about?' Chris said, groggily.

'Someone's trying to get in!' Sebastian answered in a falsely urgent whisper.

In the back garden Chris stood in his underwear looking around: He had picked up a knife from the kitchen as a weapon, and Sebastian, as he planned beforehand, had picked up a heavy cooking pan.

'I see him' Sebastian said, and as Chris turned to look Sebastian raised the cooking pan and then he brought it down on the top of his older brother's head with a massive wallop.

The force was so great the pan bounced off Chris's skull and flew across the garden into the darkness.

Things turned out better than Sebastian had expected. Chris didn't fall; he grunted, leant over and staggered down the garden path groaning.

Sebastian had imagined having to carry or drag Chris unconscious onto the railway line, but now he could simply push him forward.

Sebastian put his arm round Chris's shoulder and led him towards the end of the garden. As Christ, staggered, moaning, Sebastian tried to calm his older brother:

'We need to get you inside, and then I'll call an ambulance.'

After they had stepped through the gap in the broken brick wall, and they were right next to tube train tracks, Chris resisted going any further.

'Where are we?'

The two brothers were right next to the track and with only a couple more steps Sebastian would be able to push his older brother onto the live electric rail.

'Just take a step further.' Sebastian insisted.

Chris didn't move, so Sebastian pushed him hard.

Chris staggered, tripped over on the edge of the iron track and fell putting his hand straight on the live rail.

Sebastian lurched back holding his breath; expecting Chris to burn up.

Nothing happened.

Sebastian couldn't believe it. No power. He realized with dismay that the London Underground must turn off the electric current to the tube lines in the dead of night when no trains are running: Sebastian hadn't thought about that.

Now Sebastian had to make sure that his brother stayed where he was until the electricity was turned back on, and if the trains started running at five or six o'clock in the morning that would be in two or three hours.

Taking off his belt – Sebastian was still dressed – he tried to push his brother's head down so that he could tie Chris's neck to the live rail.

Chris fought back and kicked Sebastian away.

'What are you trying to do?' Chris demanded.

'I'm trying to help you' Sebastian answered.

'You're trying to kill me' Chris said. Then, after fighting off his brother, and getting to his feet, Chris, still staggering, went back into the house, where he called his father, who came round see what the problem was.

Chris wanted Sebastian arrested for trying to kill him, but his father didn't want the police called. He tried to sort out the problem between his two sons.

Finally, Chris calmed down, but he refused to stay in the house anymore, because Sebastian was mad, his father said that Chris could come back home with him.

Sebastian was told by his father to ring his mother, and to go and see a doctor to get help. Obediently, Sebastian said he would do this, but really, he had absolutely no intention of doing anything his father asked: his father had deserted the family to marry a dumb, drooling secretary, and this made his father scum.

A few days earlier, before Sebastian tried to kill Chris on the railway line Sebastian had bought a very big wooden handled axe with the idea of simply hacking up his brother, his father and the smug, self-satisfied secretary that his father had married, but now Sebastian thought about how to use the axe more carefully.

He stayed up all night figuring out what he could do with it.

In the hallway the newly bought house still had its original Victorian picture rails running along each wall at a little above head height.

Cutting a broom pole to fit across the gap in the corridor and resting it on the picture rails Sebastian found it was quite easy to perch the axe with the head pointing downwards with the tip of the handle resting near to top of the front door.

He worked on the balance point, until he got it just right. When the door was opened it pushed the axe forward until it swung down in a nasty curve, and with the addition of a loop of string to guide it, Sebastian saw the axe swing down fast and straight towards the open doorway at chest height, straight into the chest of anyone walking into the house.

It was perfect.

Standing in the hallway in the bright morning sunshine Sebastian realized that he had begun to feel quite sick. He'd gotten very tired from staying up all night, fighting with Sebastian and then rigging up and testing the swinging axe, so he went up to his room to have a short nap.

When he woke up Sebastian didn't know how long he'd slept and his mouth was dry. He felt spaced out and detached. He'd been living on sugar and powered glass for about a week now and he thought that this might be starting to affect him.

He had wanted to pretend that he was mentally ill in case anyone ever accused him of killing his brother, but perhaps he had carried things a little too far. Trying to live off just sugar and water and ground glass wasn't good for you.

Still, Sebastian considered his plan perfect. He would call his brother and tell him that he was sorry and ask to meet Chris at the house.

Sebastian saw it all.

He would be outside in the street waiting when Chris and their father arrived. After saying hello Sebastian would turn and walk casually down the front path and then go into the house through the front door. The opening door would unbalance the axe. The blade of the axe would hit him in the chest and he would collapse bleeding.

To help his injured brother Chris would take the axe out of Sebastian's chest putting his fingerprints on the handle.

Crying out for help Sebastian would get Chris to call for an ambulance – Sebastian would be bleeding badly and be unable to move.

As Chris began talking on the phone to the emergency services operator Sebastian would start screaming.

'You've killed me. I'm dying why did you try to kill me?'

If Chris kept the phone call going Sebastian would keep making accusations and if Chris stopped Sebastian from shouting out that he was being murdered this would condemn Chris, because it would look like Chris was trying to stop Sebastian from telling the truth. The call operator would always think that Chris had attacked Sebastian with the axe.

The plan was a good one. Sebastian felt no guilt about putting things right in this way.

In prison Chris would have plenty of time to think about what he had done to Sebastian.

Chris had betrayed Sebastian and their mother by deserting them during the divorce, and what Chris had done was more than wrong, because a brother should always be loyal to a brother.

Far worse than his failed loyalty Chris had hurt their mother by going with their father, and this was unforgiveable. Chris deserved to suffer for years on end, because like their father, Chris was too ignorant and selfish to see the harm he had done to the family.

Chris needed to be punished.

Feeling very tired Sebastian didn't have the energy to get up from his bed to phone his brother. He decided to rest and he decided that his plan could wait until later.

Sebastian closed his eyes again.

He had started to feel cold, but as his mind drifted into darkness Sebastian did not think that he was dying, he thought he was going back to sleep.

How this short story links to *The Problem of Thor Bridge*

Sebastian, due to jealousy, contrives to kill himself, and make it look like he was murdered by the person he is jealous of; as in *Thor Bridge*. Sebastian uses a weapon controlled by a piece of string to do this, as in *Thor Bridge*. The Sherlock Holmes story provides material for the new story. Some elements have been transposed, but it is new story, with characters and setting that make it original.

Originality rests not in creating something that has no links to previous sources, but by using ingredients from a range of sources to make a story that is unique. This is what jig-sawing offers as a creative technique.

Defining Yourself as a Writer

Before you undertake any sort of complex task it's a good idea to consider the resources you have. Do you have what you need to get the job done? If you want to be a successful writer then assessing your writing ability, your narrative knowledge, your storytelling skills level, and identifying the type of stories you want to write is important.

Use the lists and questions below to assess your present position as a writer; see what you need to learn now and perhaps come back to this list in a year's time and consider what has improved and what still needs to be developed.

Do you have these writing skills?
Control of grammar, punctuation and spelling
An extensive vocabulary
Understanding of writing style, structure and viewpoint
Experience of non-fiction writing: journalism, advertising
Experience of specialist writing: academic, business or technical
Experience of fiction writing: short and long stories

What's your commitment to writing?
Your enthusiasm?
Your stamina?
Do you make time to write?
Can you resist distractions?
What's been your response to rejection?
What's been your response to success?

Are you a storyteller?
Do you have a strong predisposition to storytelling?
Can you identify your key motivation as a storyteller?
What's your personal taste as a storyteller?
Have you found your 'voice' as a storyteller?
Can you jig-saw to create stories?
Do you undertake research to develop stories?

Do you understand narrative?
Do you understand a range of story structures?
Can you use storytelling terminology to develop your ideas?
Can you structure a treatment for a story into a plan for a successful novel?

The questions above are about your writing and your storytelling ability. The following questions are about you and what you use to create stories that are meaningful and important to you.

What aspects of your identity do you use to create stories?

- Cultural background
- Social background
- Social history
- Family history
- National history

What elements of your personal history and relationships do you use to create stories?

- Parents
- Siblings
- Friends
- Lovers/Partners
- Colleagues
- Acquaintances

What elements of your gender and sexuality do you use to create stories?

- Gender
- Social orientation
- Social expectations
- Personal experience

Of course writers need technical writing skills and highly developed storytelling skills, but in the end what drives a writer is the fact that their stories express something personal and deeply important to themselves as a person. A writer's stories may be mainstream popular fiction, but whatever the genre or style they are in, they are also, in some way, very personal. If you start trying to write but feel the energy and enthusiasm running low then this may be because you haven't found and identified the source that will keep you working as a writer. When literary studies and biographies discuss a writer's themes, they're often talking about a writer's personal motivations. If you can find your personal motivations, your voice, then this will sustain you as a writer and it's a good idea to think about this matter in a focused way rather than simply leaving it floating. Why do you want to write? How do you want to define yourself as a writer?

Deciding to be a writer

It may seem very pretensions to declare yourself to be 'a writer' when you have nothing published and this kind of statement might be one to avoid making in public. However, if you want to be a writer then you have to commit to making a conscious, sustained and determined effort to be a writer: a process that is likely to take several years. Writing and storytelling skills just won't develop unless they are worked on.

If you only give yourself a couple of weeks, or a couple of months, to 'try your hand at being a writer', then this meager, short-term plan, is, more likely than not, going to fail. The right thing to do is to decide to be a writer and commit yourself to the work that is needed to achieve your ambition.

Good writing

The first thing to set in place on the route to becoming a writer is the recognition of what good writing is.

What is required for good writing, more often than not, is simplicity and clarity. This aim may well sound too simple to be true - to be all that's required – but in fact the skill of clarity is not that easily mastered. This is because what 'good writing' means is *precision*: stating directly and succinctly what happens in a story and having dialogue that easily carries both plot and character. What makes this task difficult to accomplish is that when someone starts to write their story ideas are unclear, their writing skills in terms of structure, style, grammar, spelling and punctuation aren't fully developed, and so what gets put on paper is confused. Sentences aren't completely coherent, paragraphs lack purpose, and as a piece of writing grows longer the many small faults multiply until they become a severe problem, and what's essential to a good story - clear effective storytelling - is lost within a myriad of weaknesses.

Complexity in a story is not based on the complexity of the writing, but on the situations that are set up, how the characters are portrayed and a complex story can only benefit from careful, clear telling. Even very stylized prose tells the story, and it's the story that underpins every word and sentence on the page, and it's this skill of precision that the new writer needs to develop. (Of course there are examples of non-narrative writing, experimental styles, but here, in this book, the focus is on the task of novel writing as storytelling.)

The basics: grammar and punctuation

No matter how able the writer, no matter how experienced the writer, no one knows the spelling of every word and every writer will have questions about the correctness of what they have written in terms of grammar and punctuation. Keeping dictionaries, thesauruses and books on punctuation and grammar to hand are not signs of weakness or incompetence; they're invaluable tools. Louis De Bernieres, the author of the highly successful novel, *Captain Corelli's Mandolin*, was asked to design a piece of furniture that would be essential to him. Louis De Bernieres' response was to create a portable bookcase, which he could use to trolley around all the reference books he needed for his writing.

Also, actual hardcopy reference books, might well be a better choice than searching the internet to check and confirm things, because using the internet leads to browsing and much time can be consumed while the writing is still waiting to be done.

Why not start with writing but not creative writing?

Many people become fiction writers after they have worked in journalism, and Charles Dickens, George Orwell, Carl Hiassen, John Sandford, Michael Connelly and Bernard Cornwell are some examples of this route from journalist to novelist.

Journalism teaches a writer to gather the facts, structure them into a concise recounting of events, write the story to a set style, for a specific publication, to a precise word count, and to meet a timed deadline for getting the work done. This makes journalism a terrific training ground for a fiction writer. Non-fiction, journalistic writing challenges are not too daunting or too precious, The story material is gathered by the writer, just as this needs to be done to create a fictional narrative, and then these elements are written up into a clear coherent story.

As a former journalist the author Bernard Cornwell is able to write to a high standard and produce more than one novel a year: the same is true of Michael Connelly. They have benefited greatly from their first profession.

Besides journalism, and advertising copywriting, an aspiring writer could write film or book reviews, or keep a journal, or undertake business or academic writing, all of which will provide a non-fiction environment in which to develop. Just as musicians practice so writers need to practice. Similarly musicians' learn by performing the music of others and this gives them the skills and understanding necessary to develop their own work. The same is true for someone who wants to be an author: it's far easier to develop your writing abilities if you don't have to wrestle at the same time with the intricacies of your own fictional events; your own plots, characters and settings.

Learning from reading

It has been said that *every writer is a reader*, which expresses the sentiment that a love of books, of reading, will be the touchstone that leads someone to want to be a writer. This is likely to be true in many cases, but it is possible to a get a more certain and more direct return from carefully studying writing, rather than just reading novels for enjoyment.

On a day-to-day basis people read quickly, skimming across the individual words, sentences and paragraphs, and their thoughts are not concentrating on the writing style, or on the writing skills of the author; the reader is overtaken by the images and narratives that the book creates. In order to see how a piece of writing is constructed it is necessary to slow down the reading process and there are a few easy ways to do this:

- Read a book aloud so that you have to clearly form each word

- Listen to a novel as an audio book where the words are carefully and professionally read.

- Choose a piece of writing from a book and type it out in full, so that every aspect of grammar, punctuation and spelling is repeated by you

Using any of these methods of reading, being in contact with the words on the page, will offer you a stronger sense of how a piece of writing has been put together and how the story is being told.

The writer, Hunter S. Thompson, began his writing career typing and re-typing, F. Scott Fitzgerald's, *The Great Gatsby*. This was not once but many times. Thompson does not write in Fitzgerald's style, but the correspondences are clear; a desire to analyze situations beyond the present circumstances; to depict events as part of larger whole, the use of commentary to describe and delineate characters. Hunter S. Thompson developed his own signature style of writing, known as *Gonzo*, but he benefitted from learning to write through a very close and specific study of F. Scott Fitzgerald's writing technique.

Beyond the writings of others and in relation to your own work:

- Read your own writing aloud, or record it, and listen back to it. You can use text to speech on a computer to hear your own work.

- Have others read aloud what you have written so that you can hear it said by others

Using either of the options above will enable you to carefully hear the words exactly as they have been put down on paper, rather than as you might normally speed through them in silent-reading, and the effect of this will be twofold:

- Firstly, the quality and detail of what you have written will come through if the writing is good, but if it is not, you will sense the gaps, misunderstandings and poor expression that you need to return to in order to re-write and improve.

- Secondly, you will experience what you have written as though you are not the author, and from this outside perspective you will be able to sense how your story is working in terms of story, style and emotion.

Make time to create stories and make time to write

The novelist William Burroughs made the observation that if you're going to be a writer you're going to spend a large part of your life on your own. This may make the task of writing sound somewhat punitive, but to be a writer you do have to give a significant amount of time to your writing.

The Oscar winning screenwriter, William Goldman, has noted that the most difficult thing for a writer to protect is their writing time. So, it's essential for a new writer to have a structure and a schedule for when they write, because there are always everyday pressures and commitments that continually work against this.

In terms of keeping a pattern, and a sustained effort in their work, different writers organize their time in different ways. Maya Angelou writes new material in the morning, teaches in the day and corrects her work in the evening. Tennessee Williams and Woody Allen were, and are respectively, morning writers, and the Japanese author Yukio Mishima was able to start his writing at midnight and would complete a novel in six to nine months: starting at midnight suited him.

In terms of having a place to write, to get away from distractions, the authors, Virginia Woolf, George Bernard Shaw and Roald Dahl, each had an isolated place - a shed, a hut, a lodge, a hideaway - in which they could get away from day to day interruptions and get on with their writing. Some writers, such as Norman Mailer and William Goldman kept a small office in which to get their work done.

What seems to be true of almost all writers is that they establish a pattern and habit for their work and this helps them in what they do.

It might be argued that the idea of setting a specific time slot each day to write is too restrictive, because a person needs inspiration to be able to start work. However, to wait to start work because you're hoping for inspiration is a far too much of a mercurial option to use if you want to be a committed author.

Joyce Carol Oates has written over thirty novels and made the observation that when you sit down to write you may not feel like writing, but by starting to write the desire to write will come; a writer needs to develop the habit of writing even if they don't feel like it, and this will support, rather than hinder creative work.

Looking at the benefits of regular writing it is easy to see the influence it will have on your skills. If you were to write just an hour a day over the course of a year and even if you had quite a few days off – not writing - you would still have done over three hundred hours of writing work. Extending this to two or even three hours a day would give you six hundred to nine hundred hours of experience. A new writer needs to commit to being a writer, and most of all, making the time needed to do this.

Choosing what to write

The general advice for those starting to write, the question of choosing what type of story is often; *write what you know*. This does seem helpful, because it means creating stories from the material that the writer has at hand. However, it also seems to want to limit people to writing memoirs, autobiography or roman à clef. The advice that would seem preferable is to *use what you know* and from this material you can create a wide range of stories, once you have developed your jig-sawing technique. What you are looking to use in your writing is not specific biographical information; who you are, where you live, but what you know, about people, places, and events.

As an example of using what you know rather than details of your own life and biography, Patricia Highsmith, an American author, nearly always wrote crime stories, but she had little or no interest in actual police procedures or legal matters. She used crime as an environment where she could create the characters she was interested in. If she had been advised to write *what you know*, what she might have written would have been stories of college life and the literary world. Instead she used *what she knew about people* to fashion a large number of suspense crime novels. Building a fictional world from what you know is certainly a key to success, but it can't simply be a recounting or re-working of your autobiographical setting and events.

Sometimes a new writer makes a choice to write in a specific style, or to choose a subject, that they feel is worthy: literature, potentially important subjects, socially significant writing. It's good to aspire to great work, to hope that what you write will have a social relevance, but to set that as a controlling idea, which then severely limits your creative options, is more likely to make the idea of writing a significant literary work a barrier, rather than a route to success.

Don't be impressed by literary merit for its own sake, and don't try to write in a style or a type of book that doesn't really suit you.

For instance, if you want to write romantic comedies, then write romantic comedies. And remember, while the romance might well look like a lowbrow form, didn't William Shakespeare, Oscar Wilde, Richard Sheridan and Molière, all write romantic comedies? Also, isn't the enduringly popular *and* highly esteemed author, Jane Austen, a writer of romantic comedies?

Avoiding, or being worried about writing a type of story, because it superficially appears less serious than other work, is likely to be a wrong choice to make. Choose what suits you as a writer.

As an author you should feel free to try out different genres and styles, until you discover what really matches and excites your creativity; never feel that have to write to an esoteric literary standard, if that's not to your taste.

In the end, the key to choosing what you should be writing may well be in waiting for a while before deciding what your taste is. An author should always try writing in different styles and to write stories within different genres, and then, only after a number of short pieces, consider which area of writing seems the most fruitful.

Then, and only when you're confident and ready, should you move on to working on a full novel. Success in writing rests in knowing your skills and ability; being sure that what you choose to write is the best choice for you, and this knowledge takes time to develop.

A problem to avoid: setting the barrier too high

A first novel is started with excitement and enthusiasm. It's a joy to begin. Then the writing falters, there's a pause, a longer pause and then the work has effectively stalled. A writer may tell themselves that they're still writing, but the idea is drained out and the book is never finished. Why has this happened?

It may well be good to be ambitious in any field that you wish to succeed in but to start with the full-length novel is far too much of a challenge. A composer doesn't start with a full orchestral symphony; they start on smaller pieces and develop. Start with short pieces; sketches, notes, descriptions, trial chapters.

If spending time writing short pieces seems like an unnecessary expenditure of time and effort, then it may be best to see this sort of work as storing up good material for future use. An author can use the setting, plot and characters from a short story and later in their career build this into a full novel. Joseph Conrad, began with short stories, then later, successfully reworked elements of his short stories into full-length books.

A problem to avoid: the writing stops

Besides setting the barrier too high, and wanting to write a whole novel before they're ready for it, an inexperienced writer will try to rely on what might be called *gushing*; short intense periods of inspiration and excitement when ideas flow out. This kind of writing is very enjoyable and feels extremely productive, but it will not sustain a long writing project, which instead needs to be planned and pushed forward with a conscientious effort. A writer needs to keep going and this stamina is not based on inspiration, but on writing ability: the skill needed to turn ideas into written words.

The most well-know example of the inspired novel, written in two weeks, is *On The Road*. The success of this book suggests that gushing will produce stupendous results. Looking more closely at the history of the book it's been made clear that the first draft was re-worked, and re-written by Jack Kerouac, and this was an extensive process, taking several years. The single intensive process to produce a high quality book like *On The Road* is a myth. Don't rely on a burst of inspiration for your writing; it's too haphazard and uncertain.

A problem created by others: the talent challenge

Some of the books on writing and sometimes industry professionals identify talent as the one thing that you can't learn and either you have talent or you don't

The view to take, due to this question – *do or don't I have talent* - is to ignore it, because testing yourself for talent is an unnecessary trial to put yourself under. Instead, it is best to focus on developing the skills needed to create stories and on learning how to write well. If you want to ask yourself if you have talent then wait a few years before you start worrying about this question, and in fact another common tip for writers gives us the answer in terms of creative work: *It's one percent inspiration and ninety-nine percent perspiration* – talent will grow with work.

Getting a second opinion

Your friends and family may well want to support you in your writing, but they are not the people who can give you a second opinion on a piece of your work if they have no writing skills on which they can base their advice.

The manuscripts for novels submitted to literary agents and publishers are judged on whether or not the company is interested in supporting or publishing the work. Agents, and especially publishers are not there to give an author advice on writing, but to make a judgment as to the commercial potential of what they read: this does not help a new writer. A rejection by a publishing house is not a measure of a book's quality, only its assumed financial viability.

The correct way for a writer to seek advice is have their work read by someone who is knowledgeable about the field. Someone who is professional in their judgment, but also sympathetic to the author's aims. This knowledgeable professional person is the one in a position to be able to suggest what might be done to improve the work that's been produced.

There are book editors who can read a work and consider it in relation to what it offers without needing to put forward their own version of the story that's being told. They can look at the details; the narrative structure, the storytelling, and the quality of expression used by the writer, and then this editor can competently feedback on how the story and the writing style comes across. This is the relationship a writer needs to test and assess their work: not friends and family.

For many writers a supportive professional relationship is important, even essential, because they need a second opinion in order to be able to look at their work from an outside perspective. Finding the person who can give a reliable and supportive second opinion can be difficult, but a writer will know they have found a suitable supporter when this person asks the questions and makes the comments about the work that the writer themselves is thinking. The writer and the knowledgeable, trained reader, will both recognize what is good writing, what is weak, what is clear, and what is unclear and what needs to be changed.

When the first draft is done a writer can benefit greatly from support, because the re-writing process can either improve or damage a work. So, good, knowledgeable, support and advice is a welcome chance to share worries, discuss ideas and decide what to do next.

The idea of the isolated writer is one part of the writing process, it's the major creative, first draft stage, but re-writing and editing will benefit from a second opinion.

In summary: in order to define yourself as a writer, try to do the following:

- Learn how to jig-saw. Start with stories based on fact, then take on more individual projects. The more you work on creating stories the better you will become.

- Learn how to recognize material; get into the habit of storing events, people, places, things you have read, and things you have seen so that you have the material in your head to jig-saw and create stories.

- Recognize what good writing is and make it your aim to achieve this standard of work.

- Read your own work aloud so you can hear it from an outsider's perspective. Skimming over what you have written and simply accepting that it is, 'good enough' will lead to the acceptance of poor writing

- Transcribe the work of others to understand how other authors write

- Start writing non-fiction: journalism, reviews, journals, business or academic writing. This allows you to practice to your writing ability without worrying about creativity

- Research for story material: from life, from fiction, from non-fiction.

- Write short pieces at the start of your writing career and avoid taking on large works that are more likely to fail.

- Don't start on a long work until you have the experience and are able to plan out the story of a long book with an outline and chapter breakdown.

- Produce a chapter-by-chapter breakdown before committing to writing the whole novel

- Find an informed experienced person to give you feedback and support for your revising and re-writing.

- Don't fix your mind upon being one particular type of writer until you have several years' experience

Storytelling Technique

Structuring Your Novel
A story might be imagined by the prospective writer with many exciting events, multiple crises, rising complications, complex conflicts, but that is not enough to make it a satisfying story. Without a coherent overall structure a long story will start to feel chaotic and pointless. A story needs an overarching dynamic; a sense that the story has meaningful dramatic development, a clearly established through-line: a beginning, middle and end.

If you've ever had the experience of listening to someone tell a story and it seems to have a lot of details that are unnecessary, it drifts and it's not clear what is happening; who's doing what or why, then this is because the teller didn't establish a clear structure: the teller might understand the story for themselves, but they aren't explaining it properly to the listener so that the story is clearly laid out and understandable.

In a novel the reader needs to understand the setting, the identity of major characters and their motivations, and the dynamics of the plot, in order to follow a story and to become involved. To develop a basic dramatic structure for your novel before moving to a chapter breakdown a writer might consider the usefulness of the classic three-act dramatic structure that is outlined below.

Three-act dramatic structure

Act One
At the start of the book establish the situation and the central characters; don't confuse the reader, rather put them in a situation with understandable elements. Even if the story holds a mystery or a secret it still needs to be clear what the setting is and who the major characters are.

The impetus for a story is created by a disrupting incident/inciting incident. This is the event that motivates the main character to take action. In a crime fiction/whodunit, the inciting incident is almost always a murder or the discovery of a previously concealed murder, which incites the investigator/detective to take action.

In Act One, and also for the remainder of the story, the main character takes action with a clear impetus, based on the inciting incident. They want to do something and the reader follows this motivation. In the Dan Brown books, *The Da Vinci Code* and *Angels and Demons*, the reader follows the main protagonist Robert Langdon as he discovers and deciphers clues in order to solve murders and kidnappings. The inciting incident is the first murder.

Without a clear motivation a novel sags: it's not going anywhere. A book like *The Reader,* written by Bernhard Schlink, has no blasting guns or car chases, but the main protagonist, the fifteen year-old Michael Berg wants to find out the history, the background that led Hannah Schmitz to accept her role as a concentration camp guard. This is the through-line for the book, and all the other events in Michael's life are minimized so that the novel is structured to follow his investigation and his relationship with Hannah. If the book involved the story of Michael's legal career, the history of his family, or even extensive details of Hannah's life, then it would lose focus, expanding in length, while crucially at the same time losing the book's impetus as a compelling story about the relationship between two people; seen from one person's perspective.

Above all else, as a story develops, the main protagonist faces challenges, external obstacles and internal moral complications; the main character makes decisions, take action. What is essential is that the protagonist faces conflicts and complications, and by the end of Act One this reaches a climax.

In *The Reader,* Act one is concerned with the love affair between the young Martin Berg and Hannah. This ends in a crisis when Hannah leaves Martin.

Act Two

After the trials and tribulations of the first act of the story the protagonist faces, in the second act, a new set of situations with rising challenges, conflicts, dangers and decisions. By the end of act two the protagonist takes decisive action to solve their problem and to get what they want, but this does not work. This then pushes the story towards its climax.

In Leo Tolstoy's *Anna Karenina,* in the first act, Anna, who is married, begins an affair with Count Vronsky. To avoid the stigma the couple face living in Russian society they move away from St Petersburg. The book might end at this point, at the end of the first act, with everything happily resolved: Anna and Vronsky live happily ever after. However, complications carry the story forward.

In act two Anna and Vronsky find that they can't live happily together in isolation, so they return to the society life of St Petersburg, and Anna suffers because she is stigmatized and effectively punished for leaving her husband and having an affair. These complications, which make up act two, bring the story to its climax in act three; where Anna responds to being socially stigmatized.

In *The Reader*, Act One is the love affair and Act Two is Michael rebuilding his life without Hannah until he sees her again; on trial for murder.

Act Three
Here, the protagonist/s face their toughest challenge and they finally face a very difficult situation where they will succeed or fail. In the crime story the investigator will face their foe, and the couple in a happily ending romance will typically break and then rejoin, and this will be, above all else, climatic and immediate.

In Donna Tartt's *The Secret History*, a group of college friends have successfully hidden a murder from the police in the second part of the story. (The first part is the situation leading up to the murder.) Then in the final part/act three the group cannot cope with the stresses and guilt that their evasion from the police has created and this leads to a crisis, which then changes the future lives of all the characters. This crisis, takes place as immediate action, building towards a violent event.

In *The Reader*, in Act Three, Peter is a successful lawyer, and Hannah is in prison. His major conflict is whether or not he should contact her. He still loves her, but she has been convicted of murder, and as a lawyer he should believe in justice. Peter's decision, to stay away from Hannah or go to her, is the crux of his story and brings the reader to the same point of crisis.

Conclusion – coda
In this part of the story, which might be only one or two paragraphs in a novel, or sometimes a chapter, success or failure is acknowledged and the tensions and dangers created by the disrupting incident have been overcome by the final climax.

For the characters in *The Secret History* this coda presents glimpses of their lives after they leave college and the damage that committing murder has wrought upon them.

In *The Reader*, after Peter has resolved his crisis with Hannah in Act Three, he makes a trip to New York to visit the daughter of one of the witnesses who spoke against Hannah at the trial. This is a more contemplative episode than the climax, and allows for the issues of the crime and the relationship between Hannah and Peter to be seen in a wider perspective. The coda does not introduce a new crisis, and part of the resolution is the passing of an object, formerly owned by Hannah to the daughter. This is a closing event; it signals an ending.

Below is a more detailed example of a three-act story structure:

The story of the feature film *Witness* is set in contemporary America in the religious Amish community where there is a strong moral order. This is thematically contrasted with the cynicism, violence and corruption of secular mainstream American society

Prologue: Rachel Lapp is an Amish woman. Her husband has died. This prologue, set mainly at the funeral, clearly establishes the Amish community and Rachel's place within it. She is expected to re-marry and continue her religious life.

Disrupting incident: After the funeral Rachel travels with her son, Josef, to visit relatives. Josef witnesses a murder. This crime disrupts the initial plan. Rachel and Josef have to stay in the secular world while the crime is investigated.

The cop dealing with the case is John Book; he is secular and cynical and this brings him into conflict with Rachel. The major plot of the film is to solve the crime, the secondary plot line is John and Rachel falling in love; while being separated by the types of lives they lead: secular and religious.

Act One: John Book tries to catch the murderer. However, when it becomes clear that the killer is a police officer, John, Rachel and Josef are put in great jeopardy, and then John Book is shot and badly wounded. To find shelter and hide, John, Joseph and Rachel flee to the relative safety of the Amish community.

Act Two: As John Book recovers from his gunshot wound. His attraction to Rachel grows. This causes tension between Rachel and the Amish community. Rachel has brought a violent man into her home, and because of her own attraction to John, she is censured by the Amish leaders for having a sinful relationship. John and Rachel become lovers, but this idyll is broken when the killer and his partner find out where John is hiding.

Act Three: Climax. In an extended shoot out John Book kills the murderer and his partner.

Conclusion: Coda. John and Rachel are strongly attracted, but John leaves Rachel to return to his duties.

The work of writing a film like *Witness* is to create a plot idea and then give it a satisfying structure, which helps the audience understand and become involved in the drama. The three-act structure is used to shape a story; focusing on what is essential, making sure that it remains suspenseful and dramatic; avoiding events that have no real bearing on the main story.

A writer might start with a more straightforward three-act structure to their first novel and either stay with this model, or use a more complex structure.

Catch-22 has a standard short chapter structure, there is a central narrative that threads through it, but there are many storylines and they are not laid out in a chronological order: they are revealed in bits and pieces, the end at the beginning, the same incident from a different viewpoint and the same incident repeated.

This book is a complex work; it offers a structure with each chapter being related to a particular character, and each chapter offering comic, insightful and surprising episodes. The large compendium of characters and its setting in a chaotic war time environment justifies the unusual structure – each chapter offers a range of crisis and climaxes, but this structure would not necessarily suit a book with a single character facing a single focused challenge.

Chapter Structure: A, B and C Storylines

The three-act structure is used in many stories, but another way of considering how to plan out and tell the story of a novel is to work out the chapter structure and the use of point of view in some detail.

In the novel the chapter is a structuring device; each chapter containing a significant set of events, which at the end of each chapter moves the story on. The chapter also creates a sense of pace for the story; each chapter taking the story through a period of time, each chapter heading towards a solution to the problem set at the start of the book.

Rather than a single structure one can also see the novel as a number of storylines. There may be only an A story, following a single character, taking only their point of view, or there may also be a B, C, or D, story, where the point of view shifts to other characters.

The use of changing point of view, shifting between which character's story is being told, is frequently used in popular fiction. With the majority of books being written in the third person to allow for a range of different viewpoints to be taken without confusing the reader.

This approach to structuring a novel allows for the writer to choose the most important elements of the story and above all else develop a range of characters. Tension is created when the aims of different characters come into conflict and this tension is what makes a story involving and dramatic to the reader. What makes each storyline work as part of a coherent dramatic structure is that the separate the A, B, and C, plots are related, and the crisis and climax of the novel brings these events together, and the story arc of all the major characters to conclusion.

Below are three examples of novels where character viewpoint is changed between chapters. Two are written in the third person, one is written in the first person. A new writer might consider these three approaches to structuring a novel when deciding on the use of viewpoint and the planned length of their book: the intended word count being very important to decide on, because the higher the word count, the longer to write and to finish the novel. With, as a guideline for the writing time, a year for a 40,000 word book, and three or four years, or even more, for a book over 120,000 words.

Black Sunday by Thomas Harris
26 Chapters - 60,000 words approx.

Plot Summary: USA. 1977. Martin Lander, a damaged Vietnam veteran plans a terrorist attack. He is assisted by two middle-eastern terrorists, Dahlia Iyad, and Mohammad Fasil. Trying to track down the terrorists is an Isreali secret service officer, Kabakov. Other characters help Kabakov; Rachel Bauman, Edie Stiles, Jack Renfro.

Most novels, which might be classed as popular fiction, follow a similar chapter structure to *Black Sunday*: a commercial novel is usually between 40,000 to 60,000 words in length, with twenty to thirty short chapters of two to three thousand words each.

Below is the chapter list for *Black Sunday*, noting the point of view of the character for each chapter.

1. Dahlia Iyad
2. Martin Lander
3. Kabakov
4. Mohammad Fasil
5. Martin Lander
6. Dahlia Iyad
7. Kabakov
8. Dahlia Iyad
9. Kabakov
10. Rachel Bauman

11. Kabakov
12. Dahlia Iyad
13. Kabakov
14. Rachel Bauman
15. Martin Lander
16. Edie Stiles
17. Jack Renfro
18. Martin Lander
19. Muhammad Fasil
20. Kabakov
21. Abdel Awad
22. Kabakov
23. Kabakov
24. Martin Lander
25. Kabakov
26. Kabakov

Written in the third person, *Black Sunday* follows all the major characters. In terms of viewpoint the thinking of the major characters is made clear in the various chapters that follow their actions. In each chapter only one character's point of view is given dominance; their thoughts are shared with the reader. No characters are hidden from the reader in terms of their identity or role in the story; there is no mystery in terms of who people are – the reader understands what is being planned and what people's motives are.

When starting to write there's often a sense that 'giving the plot away, has to be avoided, so characters and events need to be hidden. In *Black Sunday*, the terrorist plan is known (if not in every detail) and the tension is: will it be successful? Complications add further tension. In revealing the struggles and goals of the characters the story remains involving; it's not a mystery what the protagonists are doing. For *Black Sunday*, it's a question of who will succeed and who will fail. A story with a conflict, different characters wanting different things, will carry the reader along with the unfolding events; concealing and confusing the reader can make them feel outside the story because they simply don't know what's going on.

Black Sunday is plotted as an investigation/thriller with the detective/secret agent Kabakov following the clues to identify and then catch the criminals. Kabakov is the 'hero' of the story and Martin Lander, Dahlia Iyad and Mohammed Fasil, the 'villains'. The benefits of changing point of view, rather than staying solely with Kabakov, are because it makes it possible to carry a complex plot, keeping to the highlights of the drama, while also maintaining Kabakov as a central character. Kabakov's viewpoint dominates the climax and the ending of the book. Dahlia Iyad is the viewpoint character in several chapters, but crucially, these chapters are used to describe Martin Lander and his abnormal behavior: this ensures that Martin Lander's role as the arch protagonist is maintained, while he is at an emotional distance from the reader.

However, something that might appear out of place in the chapter structure is that two of the chapters are from Rachel Bauman's perspective. She is a doctor who has a relationship with Kabakov. Also, two chapters feature the FBI agent Jack Renfro, who is the agent in charge of security where the attack will take place. These chapters, from the viewpoint of secondary characters, allow for plot information to be conveyed to the reader, and they also provide comment on Kabakov in order to explore his motives and back story. These chapters give the point of view of essentially minor characters, but they are useful to the story, because they convey major elements of the plotting and develop relationships, and so they are not out of place. One might argue that the relationship between Kabakov and Rachel Bauman slows the story down, it is not essential to the main plot, which is the planned bombing, but this is really a question of personal preference; the author wanted to structure the story to show the relationship between these two characters, and crucially Rachel Bauman is brought into the hunt for the terrorists; she has to be included in the main story, or the reader would not understand how Kabakov found Martin Lander.

For a new novel, if an author had a story that needed to follow two or more sets of characters in parallel action – moving back and forth between different elements of the plot, then *Black Sunday*, a work of popular fiction, could well provide a suitable model. This type of book can be a useful guide when moving from a story written in outline to a plan for a book with structured chapters.

What would be used to prepare a new and different novel is the structure of *Black Sunday*, not its plot. This structure, third person, multiple viewpoint, A, B, and C storylines, might be used for any type of story: a comedy, a domestic drama, a SF fantasy.

For a new writer, rather than leaving the length of a book undecided it can be best to plan to write a book of 40,000 to 60,000 words, a standard length novel. In this structure the plot is divided into clearly defined elements, which would then be written in chapters of 2,000/3,000 words each. In this plan, roughly eight chapters would establish the story, fourteen chapters would develop the story, forming the center of the book, and the remaining eight chapters would bring the story to its climax and conclusion. This is a clear narrative structure, and through a process of trial and error, an outline for a new story can be matched to a chapter plan, and all of this offers a far more precise guide for successfully finishing a novel than just starting to write the first page having no idea where the story is going.

Also, during the writing of a book, if you are using a chapter plan, it is possible to tell if the writing is going well, because the novel is progressing according to the planning, or if this plan is not working it is possible to stop writing, re-plan the plot and/or the chapter structure of the novel. A novel can easily end up being over-written and badly structured if there is no clear sequence of events divided into chapters; the writer needs an overview, a chapter plan, to keep the novel clear and dramatic.

Using a pre-existent book as a model for your own work is a question of identifying a book that tells a story with a similar numbers of characters, with a plot going over a similar period of time, and if you're writing a genre novel, then using a book in the same genre as your own work may well provide a good guide for chapter breakdown.

The main idea is to use a published and successful book structure to help you develop and shape a new and different story.

Red Dragon by Thomas Harris
54 Chapters - 120,000 words approx.

Plot Summary: Will Graham, ex-FBI agent, is asked to help in the hunt to catch the serial killer 'The Tooth Fairy', whose real name is Francis Dolarhyde. This request for Will Graham to help comes from FBI task force leader, Jack Crawford.

After writing *Black Sunday*, Thomas Harris wrote, *Red Dragon*. This second book uses the same story, chapter structure and approach to viewpoint as the first.

Written in the third person, each of the major characters has chapters from their viewpoint. The viewpoint of some secondary characters is sometimes given, but usually at the start of a chapter, before it is passed on to a major character. No characters are hidden from the reader in terms of their actions or identity – the reader knows who the killer is. The whodunit element stems from the FBI/Will Graham tracking down the serial killer, Francis Dolarhyde. However, there is no mystery as the killer is known to the reader. It is a thriller based on a hunt for a killer.

These are fivty-four chapters in the book and the viewpoint for each chapter is listed here:

1. Will Graham
2. Will Graham

3.	Will Graham
4.	Will Graham
5.	Hoyt Lewis
6.	Will Graham
7.	Will Graham
8.	Hannibal Lecter
9.	Francis Dolarhyde
10.	Will Graham
11.	Francis Dolarhyde
12.	Will Graham
13.	Will Graham
14.	Will Graham
15.	Jack Crawford
16.	Will Graham
17.	Jack Crawford
18.	Will Graham
19.	Francis Dolarhyde
20.	Freddy Lounds
21.	Freddy Lounds
22.	Will Graham
23.	Hannibal Lecter
24.	Lecter/Graham
25.	Francis Dolarhyde
26.	Francis Dolarhyde
27.	Francis Dolarhyde
28.	Francis Dolarhyde
29.	Francis Dolarhyde
30.	Will Graham
31.	Reba McClane
32.	Will Graham
33.	Francis Dolarhyde
34.	Will Graham
35.	Reba McClane
36.	Will Graham
37.	Francis Dolarhyde
38.	Francis Dolarhyde
39.	Francis Dolarhyde
40.	Will Graham
41.	Reba McClane
42.	Will Graham
43.	Will Graham
44.	Francis Dolarhyde
45.	Will Graham
46.	Francis Dolarhyde
47.	Will Graham
48.	Francis Dolarhyde
49.	Will Graham
50.	Will Graham

51.	Will Graham
52.	Will Graham
53.	Will Graham
54.	Will Graham

Red Dragon is fairly long and complex for a crime novel, and shifting to the killer for five consecutive chapters, 25-29, is the most unusual element of the story structure. The aim of these five chapters is to greatly increase the reader's understanding of the Francis Dolarhyde, and this diversion from the main plot allows for a more complex climax.

Will Graham and Dolarhyde meet only once, but because the reader understands, in depth, the motives of these two characters this chapter is especially climatic. The five chapters that describe Francis Dolarhyde's early life, make his motives and character much stronger and therefore he is a more challenging antagonist for the ex-FBI agent, Will Graham, to defeat.

Black Sunday and *Red Dragon* have the same structure, third person, multiple points of view, but one book is much longer than the other; the first being 26 chapters and the second 54 chapters. This extra length is something that a new novelist might be wary of. *Black Sunday* is a first novel, and is roughly 60,000 words, while *Red Dragon* is approximately 120,000. The time span that Thomas Harris took to research and write *Red Dragon* was seven years, and his next two books, *Silence of The Lambs*, and *Hannibal*, have similar timeframes and they are both long books.

For a writer, wanting to write their first book, a seven year commitment is a long time, whereas a shorter book, 40,000 to 60,000 words might be planned and completed in a year or two years, even if the writer is not a full-time novelist. The worst approach for a new writer might well be just to start writing, and not even have an estimation of how long a book might take to finish. The chapter plan gives the structure for the story, but it is also a vital planning document; a good plan making it possible to keep to a schedule and finish a book in a timetable that suits the author.

The other problem with a long book for a first novel is quality. This is both in terms of story, and in terms of writing. If a story goes wrong in a short book this can be fairly quick to correct; several weeks. In a long book it might take more than a year. If a book is finished and the writing quality is good; it's clear, it's expressive, the story comes across well, then the book is a success. However, if a book needs extensive revisions and re-writing, undertaking this task for a 60,000 word book is far easier than for a book of 120,000 words.

It's possible to decide on the length of novel, a long or a short book, but there is an unfair criteria in terms of getting a novel published. When a writer is established, and there is a readership for their work, then there is a demand for their books, and the tendency is for an author to write long books, which is the case with very popular writers like Stephen King and J.K. Rowling. The unfairness is that publishers would prefer shorter books from first time novelists. This is not always the case; first time novelists do publish long works, but the majority of new authors produce work within the 40,000 to 60,000 word range.

Fingersmith by Sarah Waters
17 Chapters - 150,000 words approx.

Plot Summary: Victorian London. Sue Trinder, a fingersmith, petty thief, becomes the maid servant of Maud Lilly, with the intention of tricking Maud into marrying a man who wants her fortune.

The book is in three parts:

>   Part One. First person viewpoint: Sue Trinder
>   Part Two. First person viewpoint: Lilly Maud
>   Part Three. First person viewpoint: Sue Trinder

The first person viewpoint has informal language; internal thoughts. This provides comment on what is happening, what the character is thinking, but the writing style still allows for detailed, external, 'third person' description of action and settings. It is not stream of consciousness.

This is the chapter structure of *Fingersmith*, identifying the viewpoint in each chapter and part.

1.	**Part One**	Sue Trinder
2.		Sue Trinder
3.		Sue Trinder
4.		Sue Trinder
5.		Sue Trinder
6.		Sue Trinder
7.	**Part Two**	Maud Lilly
8.		Maud Lilly
9.		Maud Lilly
10.		Maud Lilly
11.		Maud Lilly
12.		Maud Lilly
13.		Maud Lilly

14.	**Part Three**	Sue Trinder
15.		Sue Trinder
16.		Sue Trinder
17.		Sue Trinder

As a historical novel the chapter lengths in *Fingersmith* are longer and the book as a whole much longer than the majority of contemporary popular fiction. The novel is a pastiche of classic Victorian fiction such as *The Lady in White,* so that its writing style is based on this type of classical novel, rather than the modern novel. The book's length, far longer than either *Black Sunday,* or *Red Dragon,* is justified by the author's intention to follow the form of the Victorian novel.

What makes *Fingersmith* very different from either *Black Sunday* or *Red Dragon* is that Part One of the Sarah Waters' novel tells the story of the fraud from the Sue Trinder's perspective. Then Part Two re-starts the story, and tells the same story again from Lilly Maud's point of view, which is a very unusual structure – a modernist approach to fiction.

Since the story is told twice, the use of point of view is *playful*, it gives the reader insights that the characters do not share and this is the aim of the author. A reader might be irritated to have to read about exactly the same events twice, because a novel usually only tells its story once, but it is expected that this change of viewpoints in *Fingersmith*, and the precisely repeated narrative, will be enjoyed for its own sake.

This approach to the structure is also thematically valid in structuring the story, because at the start Sue Trinder and Maud Lilly do not understand each other; they misread each other's motives and feelings, but they come together later in the story. The structure of the novel allows the reader to poignantly participate in the mutual misunderstanding between the two central characters.

Structurally, and in terms of writing style, *Fingersmith* is carefully conceived, as a pastiche of a Victorian romance, and as a dramatic use of changing viewpoint, but, importantly, to signal the change from Sue Trinder to Maud Lilly's differing perspectives, the novel is divided into three distinct parts, and this split is marked by a title page announcing each new part. The three-part structure gives the reader a strong signal that a major change has happened in the story. Often a book split into parts announces a significant jump in time, but in the case of *Fingersmith* it is a shift in story viewpoint from one character to the next, and for part two, a jump back in time in order to re-start the story. If the novel was structured simply with numbered chapters one to seventeen, then the significance to the reader of the changing viewpoint three-part structure might became vague and seem like a writing mistake.

The longer chapters in *Fingersmith*, compared to the shorter chapters in either *Black Sunday* or *Red Dragon*, has a reason based on the structure of the story. The two Thomas Harris books are thrillers and each chapter covers a crucial stage in the planning for the crime or the hunt for the criminals/terrorists. These are events such as the delivery of smuggled explosives from ship to shore in *Black Sunday*, and the abduction of a news reporter in *Red Dragon*, and they are told in detailed immediate action in order to make them as action-packed and dramatic as possible.

In contrast the action in *Fingersmith* is less obviously clear cut and dramatic; events are significant to the story, Sue Trinder arriving at a house, going for a walk, looking around a room, but these are smaller events than an action thriller, and they offer a minutiae, where the focus is on the perception of the character of these events. Crucially, in terms of book structure, each low-key event wouldn't break down into a short dramatic chapter. The longer chapters in *Fingersmith* combine several events, often spread over a number of days, even weeks. This creates longer than usual chapters, because the alternative would be a novel with a high number of very short, unevenly broken chapters, and this would be a disruptive structure for the reader to follow.

The novel *The Piano Teacher*, by Elfriede Jelinek, is similar to *Fingersmith* because both use first person point of view, and the plotting is often concerned with the emotional reaction and feelings of the first-person character, rather than with large scale action-based events. However, in *The Piano Teacher* the story structure is deliberately allowed to become confused, and rather than having clear chapter breaks the text of the novel is interrupted by double asterix ** which creates a line break between unnumbered chapters/parts.

The use of the double asterixes offers an interruption to the story, it marks some sort of break, but is not a clearly numbered chapter break and does not follow a standard pattern. The author's aim in *The Piano Teacher* is to present a fragmented character and so the structure is appropriate to this story: it's an intentional confusion, but the story doesn't jump and change erratically; it's a first person novel, which uses asterix breaks to structure an episodic story which focuses on the central character's obsessive perception of their situation.

The examples of *Black Sunday*, *Red Dragon* and *Fingersmith*, show how writers makes decisions about viewpoint and how they plan chapters in order to structure their stories, and this study of pre-existent books is useful for a writer thinking about their own work. Finding a published book that provides a template for a new novel can be a great help, and will make a new writer more confident that they have made the right choice for the structure of their own book. And from this starting point they can be far more certain that their book will be written to a professional standard.

In general there are two main aims when planning a book structure:

1. Break down the plot into separate elements and work towards a chapter structure. This will make the telling of the story more coherent and allow for the length of the novel to be planned and controlled. It also means that the story can follow a dramatic three-act structure, or an A, B, C, storyline structure, or something more complex: perhaps a story with unusual jumps in temporality: moving back and forth between present and past, while mixing character viewpoint in an unexpected way, or with a minor character telling the story of the major characters, and just picking and choosing the parts of the story that they want to recount.

Many first time authors write novels with very long starts, stodgy and long central sections and then rushed endings. This front-heavy structure still tells the story, but the ending will feel hurried and unsatisfactory to the reader, because the book is padded, and quality of the plotting and characterization is vague and diminished. A novel with too much detail or one which drifts away from the main plot will make the reader feel that they a drifting; they are being given facts, shown incidents, but these don't relate to any focused plotting; the structure of the book is weak.

2. Decide on the use of viewpoint for the book. With a story being told from the viewpoint of a single character the story can usually be written either in the first person or the third person. If the story is meant to have a sense of being completely inside the mind of character, then first person is the likely choice for the book, while third person is more external, but the thoughts of the character will still be given.

With multiple characters, third person narration is the usual choice, but, as an exception, first person can be used if the aim is to tell the story by jumping from one close-up personal experience to the next.

Second person, addresses 'you' the reader and this can be used if author want to recount their story as if they are telling it directly to the reader; like a fireside story: 'Let me tell you the story of how I killed my brother.'

Some novelists do just start their novels without a fixed sense of where they are going to go in terms of all the characters and without a full plot. They structure as they go along, but what's important to understand is that this looser approach will work only if the writer has the skills at the start to keep viewpoint and chapter structure under control. They may not know the story in detail, but an author starting without an ending, such as is the case with Stephen King or Harlan Coben, will write short chapters which are consistently first person or third person. They will present the thoughts of their central characters and each chapter will have some significant action.

A story structure based on *The Count of Monte Cristo*

While a story can be structured using a pre-existing book, this can be taken further and it is possible to create an original story, developing it from a pre-existing plot and book structure.

In the breakdown below the three-part structure of *The Count of Monte Christo* has been transformed to create another story set in a different period of time. In both, the basic structure is the same: a man is betrayed by those he trusts, he is falsely accused and then escapes from prison, the innocent man then defeats the men who betrayed him.

Original Structure: *The Count of Monte Cristo* **by Alexander Dumas**

Setting: Napoleonic France

- Dante, Mondego and Danglers are officers on a trading ship

- Dante is framed by Mondego and Danglers and put in prison.

- Dante is separated from his true love, Mercedes and she is told he is dead

- Dante escapes from prison and takes possession of a fortune in gold

- Dante takes revenge on those who betrayed him

- Dante and Mercedes are reunited as a couple, and live on, in happiness, with their child

For a new novel with same structure as *The Count of Monte Christo*

Setting: Texas, Today

- Dante is a police officer in a small border town along with Mondego and Danglers

- Dante arrests two men carrying a large sum of illegal money. When Dante refuses Mondego's request to release the two men without charge, Mondego and Danglers connive to kill Dante, but when this fails Dante is arrested and imprisoned.

- Learning Dante will be killed in prison, his wife, Mercedes helps him to escape. They go on the run, taking their son with them, and they are pursued by Mondego and Danglers.

- Mondego and Danglers manage to take Mercedes and her son hostage: they will release the mother and son in return for Dante giving himself up to be killed.

- Dante returns to town, steals the money brought by the two men Dante arrested earlier. Dante uses this money as a bargaining chip in order to arrange for the safe return of his wife and son.

- At the handover to gets his son back, Dante, along with Danglers are Mondego are all killed. Mercedes rescues her son and she and the boy leave with the money.

This reworking of *The Count of Monte Christo*, uses both the structure of the original and elements of the characters and story, but the setting, and the actual events of the story will produce a new story with new different events and a different outcome.

Terminology for Storytelling

When you create a story through your imagination, through jig-sawing, this a rewarding process. To be able to set out a plot for a novel in a written outline, or in a treatment, is creatively satisfying. The planning for a novel gives you the plotting and characters for a long story, but this narrative might still end up as an unconvincing, dull, and plodding book, unless you carefully analyze your story using storytelling technique.

You need to test and refine your plot, going beyond how you first imagined it, in order to make sure that the telling of your story is as dramatically and emotionally effective as possible. Storytelling terminology will help you develop your story, and here the aim is to:

- Ensure that a plot is convincing and coherent

- Ensure that the reader becomes involved with the characters and the events in the story

- Ensure that you can use a range of approaches to storytelling to enhance the plotting, the drama and the emotion of the story

The terminology developed for studying literature is certainly useful for understanding how to write a novel, and a good dictionary or guide to literary theory is something for a writer to read and study. The slight limitation is that this terminology is used for intellectual analysis, not creative thinking. The terms below are to help the creative process and to help you judge and develop your own original story: how well it's working, what is over-predictable, where has a story become padded or unclear, how can a story be told in a way which creates more tension and interest.

Story World Conventions: Being absolutely clear how the world of a story works, what is possible and what is not, is essential to a coherent well-told narrative. There are established genres and conventions for storytelling that offer a range of models for how a story world will work, but each story has to be specifically defined and sure of its own conventions.

When a novel takes places is an unrealistic world, such as in the supernatural or the fantastic, it's obvious that 'realistic' conventions don't apply: people can live forever, people can fly, objects have magical properties, and this might suggest that a novel based in an everyday world is convention free, but each novel creates its own world, and the way this world works needs to be consistent.

In the fantasy world of the Charlaine Harris, *Sookie Stackhouse* novels, the vampires, as in the classic supernatural stories, cannot survive in the sunlight, but in Stephanie Meyer's, *Twilight* novels, vampires can live in the light. Each author is writing vampire books, but they have established different story world conventions. The reader will accept these differences, if these conventions are made clear at the start, and they don't randomly change as the plot progresses.

In the 'realistic' world of the Jane Austen novels, these seem to portray everyday life in the 1800's, but the plots take place in a story world which focuses on social etiquette and romance, while excluding issues of social poverty, religion, war, slavery. A writer should not rely on the idea that their novel represents 'real-life' to justify what it includes in the story. Instead, the author should be clear what conventions they are using to represent their fictional world to the reader.

Point of View: Whose story is being told? Does the reader know everything or are they confined to one person's point of view? Point of view can be simple or complex, but whatever the case it needs sure handling in order to be certain that the sense of narrative cohesion is maintained. Jumping or changing point of view to do something like convey a single piece of plotting would be very weak. It would be like a piece of music changing style for no reason and for just a moment.

There's a tendency for new writers to have limited control of viewpoint. They feel they need to tell a story from the viewpoint of a single character, and while there are many stories that do this successfully, it can also be the case that shifting viewpoint enriches the story and makes the storytelling more vivid.

There is also the problem with new writers writing in the third person. They often write the story through commentary; over-describing characters and commenting extensively on the action, until the reader feels like they are being led thorough the story, rather than experiencing it. Controlling point of view makes for clear and credible storytelling.

Inciting incident, disruption of equilibrium: The idea of an *inciting incident*, which could also be called a *disruption of equilibrium*, is the pivotal event near the start of a story that shifts events away from their normal path.

In the film *North by Northwest*, Roger O. Thornhill, a New York businessman, is mistaken for a secret agent, which then takes his sedentary life off course and into high adventure.

To engage the reader a story has to be about more than humdrum, everyday life. What builds a story are a series of complications that act as challenges or obstacles, or goals. A lack of inciting incident would give a story no momentum, because it is merely a flow of events. A plot, as the word suggests, creates a direction: the characters are going somewhere. The *inciting incident* is the major event that sets the plot moving forward.

In the film *Identity*, a number of travelers are trapped at an isolated motel due to flooding and heavy storms. The opening scenes of the film show how each character ends up at the motel; this represents a series of incidents which establishes the situation and characters so that the main plot of the story can take place. The major event, the disrupting incident occurs when it is discovered that there is a killer in their midst; this means that everyone is trapped at the hotel and the characters now have a number of strong motivations: to stay alive, to find the killer, to get away from the motel. Without the murder plot, all the story would have was several unhappy people waiting for a storm to pass, which might well be dull and very passive.

Back Story: There is the start of the story as it is told and there is the back story: the events that led each and every character up to the point where they join the story. Back story defines characters, sets up motivations, relationships and situations, conceals secrets, adds depth.

There's the back story for what each character has done, there's what each character knows and there's what the reader knows as they learn new things about past events and characters. The back story might be put in place by a prologue, or the back story might become clear only in the final scene. The writer needs to be sure that they are conveying what they want to of the back story, so that it is clear to the reader, but it also has to be convincingly done; simply jumping into an explanation of things can feel like the author is intruding on the action.

In Fyodor Dostoyevsky's *Crime and Punishment*, a young man commits a murder with the apparent aim of testing to see if he is a 'Napoleon'; someone who is entitled to kill others because of his individual inherent right. What emerges as the story progresses is a back story involving the young man's sister, and the man she is having to marry. Eventually, it is the relationship between brother and sister that developed long before the start of the story, as it is set out in the book, which is the crux of the novel. The back story is crucial to *Crime and Punishment*, but only gradually emerges

Back stories establish consistency and motivation; characters might develop and change, but they need to be established with a sense of having a past, a personal history before the first events in the novel.

Set up and pay off, foreshadowing: Sometimes a plot point is made and the implications of this small event for the story only becomes clear much later: story points are set up and then their significance is paid off. Set ups and pay offs create a weaving interconnection between different parts of the story and these add depth and detail to a story.

In *Red Dragon*, the FBI find a Chinese idiomatic character carved into a tree, this is the symbol for the Red Dragon, which is later shown to be a major element of the serial killer's identity. The tree-carving is a set-up which then pays off with a revelation about the killer.

Complications: A plot development will often cause a complication; an incident that affects the characters in the story and influences the events that follow. A story needs complications to give it tension and conflict. If a novel has long passages where things progress without disruption then these events may not need to be in the story. They can be left out, or the story changed to avoid long, uneventful passages.

In *The Grapes of Wrath*, the Jode family loose their farm due to debt, which is the inciting incident of the story, and it puts the family on a path to find a new life. During this journey they face many complications and challenges. The complications allow the reader to empathize with and understand the plight of the displaced family.

Reversals, turnarounds: As a story progresses the reader begins to anticipate what will happen next and in a poorly constructed story they will be correct too often, and they are likely to be disappointed as a result of this over-predictability. Readers may expect happy endings, but these cannot be reached in a clichéd, dull and easily predictable way. One technique to avoid this problem is to use a *reversal*, also known as a *turnaround*, which creates an obstacle for a character and changes how they will act.

A reversal is a very significant event which surprises the reader and sets the story on a new unexpected path. What the reader is anticipating for the story is disrupted and changed. Reversals keep the reader guessing and engaged.

Imagine the story of a couple being chased through the forest by someone intending to kill them. They come to a road and see a parked car, its doors open, the key in the ignition. For the reader the appearance of the car, just when it is needed, ready and waiting, will seem too convenient. However, if the car won't start and this delays the fleeing couple, who are then nearly caught, this reversal will add to the tension.

In Colin Dexter's, Inspector Morse detective mystery novel, *The Way Through the Woods*, Morse is looking for a missing woman. He believes that she has been murdered and buried in a wood. When a body is finally found Morse expects this to be the missing woman's corpse, but it is the body of man. This is a significant turnaround for the story; it sets the story on a new, unexpected path; who is this man, and how can he be in the grave that Morse found when expecting to find the woman?

Surprise and Suspense: A surprises make a story dynamic, because it offers the unexpected. Too many surprises may well make a story ridiculous, because they become unrealistic. A story doesn't have to rely on surprises and instead suspense is often a more enduring tension.

Suspense is created when the reader knows something that one or more of the characters do not. Using suspense can be very effective in pulling the spectator into the story.

In Donna Tartt's *The Secret History,* the fact that the main protagonists are murderers is established at the very start, and the suspense rests with a number of issues; will they be found out, what will happen to characters, and most of all, in the lead up to the killing, the reader feels a tension, a strong suspense, because they understand that one of the characters is behaving in a way that will make the others decide to kill him. In this novel giving the plot away, letting the reader know how things stand right from the first page, instead of concealing the murder, creates a stronger, more effective story.

Surprise does have a place in storytelling; there's no doubt about that; a sudden breathtaking shock can thrill a reader, but suspense which is a less familiar term, is one that can be used to enliven many scenarios.

Suspense and surprise relate to the use of *character knowledge*. Suspense gives the reader knowledge that a character or characters do not have and this knowledge gives the reader an awareness of a situation, often a danger, which in turn heightens the emotional impact of a story.

Misdirection: There are plot points that lay false trails. A reader is always be thinking ahead, trying to work out in advance how a story will end and misdirection can deliberately lead them astray and make them assume things have happened or will happen, but these turn out to be false trails.

Like complications and reversals, misdirection can add depth and detail to a story. Too much misdirection will confuse a story and undermine its sense of coherence. Almost all murder mysteries involve misdirection: they suggest that a range of people might be the criminal, but this is eventually proved incorrect.

In *Affinity,* by Sara Waters, the central character is skeptical about the ability of another character to be able to communicate with the dead; spiritualism is not considered credible. Then, slowly, but surely the central character, and by implication the reader, starts to feel that there is a supernatural element, that events can't be explained any other way. This however, is elaborate misdirection.

Raising the stakes - Risk and jeopardy: What's at stake? When the problem or the challenge for the protagonist in the story becomes more difficult, the threat more deadly, this increases the emotional tension. Raising the stakes heightens the drama.

What often makes a story dramatic is the level of risk or challenge involved. It doesn't have to be the violence or death, but it has to be important enough so that the reader can empathize with the protagonist's situation.

If in a story a man goes out to buy the Sunday papers, perhaps the only risk is that the newspaper shop has sold out of the particular Sunday paper that the man wants to buy. This story is unlikely to engage many people. Instead, if the story is about man who has to get a vital medicine for his wife and she will die unless she gets this in the next hour, there a lot is at stake, and any obstacle or complication to the man's journey will *raise the stakes* and increase the *risk* of failure so that the story becomes a life or death struggle.

In the novels written by Lee Child, the central protagonist, Jack Reacher, is shown to be super-confident with a high level of physical and mental ability. This means he can cope with most situations. He's not in danger. To put a sense of jeopardy into these novels there will often be a more vulnerable character that Jack Reacher supports and protects: a beaten woman, an old woman. These characters raise the stakes because they are in jeopardy.

Climax: A story reaches a climax and this will resolve the plot and carry the reader to a height of emotion. A climax may well need more time, in terms of page-length, than is essential for the telling of the story. There's a temptation for a new writer to write every scene, right from the first page, in great detail, but this slows down the pace of a story and can lead to the reader losing interest. The climax is where all the elements of the plot come together and this part of the book benefits from being extended because of the importance of the ending and the resolution of the story to the reader.

Unseen Action: There is unseen action; things which happen in the story which are not described in the book. Unseen action can be used for two main reasons. Firstly, to jump over events which have little or no importance to the central plot. For example, a character can be in their office getting ready to go to an airport, and then be sitting in their seat on the plane. If there's no significant story event that takes place during the journey to catch the flight there's no need to describe it. Because a writer imagines a story in detail, they might well think about events which are, in the end, not essential to the plot, and these can be dropped when the book is written.

Unseen action, also works as a useful device because the reader can fill in the plot gaps, and this can make the reader more involved in the story, as they are 'filling in the details'. This second reason for using unseen action is to have strong dramatic impact. Events are described, then, at a certain point, the reader, usually matching the thinking of a character in the story, will realize that something dramatic has happened which has not be told in the book.

In *The Narrows*, a private detective is investigating the death of a former FBI profiler, and, quite separately, in a different storyline, the FBI are investigating a murder site. What is not shown, are the killer's actions – they are unseen. The reader, like the FBI and the private investigator, are finding clues, wondering what's going on, so that the reader joins in the investigation, and this makes it more involving as a story. When the unseen action is finally understood in *The Narrows* this has a frisson and surprise.

The reader understands that the killer is deliberately setting up a trail of clues so he will be followed, not that he has made a number of mistakes, and this means that it is the FBI who need to be wary, not the killer. This new and sudden understanding gives the reader the same realization as the FBI: they're in danger, and this raises the stakes. Telling the story this way has emotional impact.

The other option, of showing what the killer does, hiring a boat for a fishing trip, carrying a corpse, is not necessarily the most dramatic or involving way to reveal the plot, and giving all the details of the story can be less intriguing for the reader. This is because figuring out unseen events brings the reader into the story.

Stereotypes: If a person reading a book thinks that the characters in it are *clichéd* in the way that they talk and behave this makes it a story based on jaded *stereotypes*, which is bad writing, because the reader should feel that a story is genuine, and original. A *clichéd* novel comes across as a re-hash of other familiar stories, usually ones which are better written.

However, and as a seeming contradiction, all stories have to have an element of stereotyping. Characters and stories are not wholly original and in fact readers like a certain familiarity with a situation and what's going to happen; readers want to recognize who is the hero and who is the villain. The balance then is to avoid what is over-familiar and what has become worn out.

To overcome the dilemma inherent in stereotyping; how to be familiar without being stale, the aim of good writing is to work with recognizable characters in a well-conceived, and well-constructed plot, where actions and reactions have an authenticity that makes them feel spontaneous and fresh. If the characters' actions and reactions appear genuinely motivated the reader accepts them as genuine and so original.

No successful dramatic character is entirely a stereotype. A character might be recognizable as a 'tough, determined cop', but this stereotype is given depth, through their background, personal history, their relationships with others, and also, in how these factors have influenced their personality.

As a further complexity in the need to use stereotypes; very successful comedy can be based on gross exaggerations and demeaning portrayals of well known character types.

Super-objective: Each character has a super-objective, a *through-line*, something that motivates them, which structures their personality and keeps them moving through the story. The super-objective for a character may be a simple statement - they want to love – but it has to be coherently defined: a person who wants to love will give love and a person who needs love will want to receive love. These are two very different super-objectives, and would make a character behave in very different ways.

The super-objective for a character might be expressed by an external goal; I want to be rich, but this is underpinned by an internal super-objective; I won't let anyone get the better of me.

In terms of super-objective the most important principal to work from is the fact that character defines what actions are taken; nothing happens in a story without a character acting and responding to their own internal dynamic. When a character makes sense, what they do makes sense and the story is likely to be convincing.

Fictional characters need to clearly defined, and they do not, in the end, have the complexity or uncertainty of real people. A writer cannot defend their character by saying that in a real life situation a person might be changeable, or might make a range of different and unclear decisions. A story character functions within a set of rules, as though they were in a game. Like a piece on a chessboard, once a character in fiction is drawn, then they can only act in a number of ways.

In the film *High Noon*, a lone sheriff who has decided to stay and protect the town from approaching gunman, stays until the end, even though no one has offered to help him. In real life a person might want to stay and fight a threat, but if everyone then lets them down, they might well change their mind and decide to leave. The fictional character is set on a course, and if they waver, then, the story falls apart. The final climatic conflict between the sheriff and the gunman would not happen if the sheriff left the town and the story would then be an anti-climax. Super-objective needs to remain in place for a fictional character.

Scene objective: A scene objective is the character's specific objective for a scene, an event in the story, which may or may not result in the outcome they want. The scene objective can't contradict the super-objective or a character's behavior would become incoherent and senseless; the scene objective will stem from the super-objective.

In *Black Sunday* the Israeli government agent, Kabakov, questions a smuggler name Muzi. Kabakov's scene objective is to find out who hired Muzi to smuggle plastic explosives. This scene objective is thwarted when Muzi is killed by an explosion during his questioning. The explosion is a plot reversal. It means that Kabakov can't get the vital information he wants know, but if his scene objective, to 'find out' was not clear then the explosion would have little apparent significance; scene objectives keep the reader following the plot, and they are tied to the character's super-objective. Kabakov's super-objective is to catch the terrorists, and his emotional reaction to Muzi's death is based on that. He is frustrated and angry because he has not got the information he wants, not because he cares for Muzi.

Character developments and character arcs: Some stories are about a profound change to a character's super-objective. Such as a character who is only out for what they can get for themselves learns to be unselfish.

In *The Secret History*, the central character begins with being overawed by a small clique of students, but at the end, he, and the reader, have come to know what these students are really like, and this effects the central character and their choices in adulthood.

Heroic idealized characters, like Jack Reacher, in the novels written by Lee Child, never really change, but in a less idealized story world the character arc matches the idea of maturity, or growth, or realization for the central the character. The internal or emotional change in the character is often identified as the thematic core of the story: what does the character learn from the story, and in turn what themes and ideas does the story convey to the reader.

Character knowledge: While there is unseen action, where the writer leaves the reader to fill in the gaps, and there is suspense where the reader knows more about a situation than some of the characters, there is also character knowledge: how much the characters in the novel know about each other's feelings and motives.

In the film *What Lies Beneath* a woman believes that she is going insane or she is seeing ghosts. Her husband appears to the wife, and to the film audience, to be supportive, loving and kind, but secretly, and unknown to the audience, he is in fact certain that his wife has found out about his affair with a young women, whom he murdered. The husband believes that his wife is being cruel to him by pretending she is mad and acting as if she is seeing a ghost of the murdered woman.

In this *What Lies Beneath* it is essential to the story structure that in the early stages of the plot the audience aren't privy to the husband's thoughts, or his back story, because it would destroy the suspense and tension of the story. The audience would know that the man was a murderer from the very start, and that the dead woman was a ghost – the wife is not mad. Instead, what the audience sees is the viewpoint of the wife toward her husband; they are not given any sense of the husband's guilty suspicions until the start of the final third of the film, and this revelation is then a powerful reversal, which builds to the climax of the story.

Story characters can have knowledge that other characters are unaware of, and also that the audience is unaware of, until there is dramatic revelation, which is also likely to be a reversal. Hidden motives can fuel a story, but these motives cannot remain entirely hidden; the secret has to come out.

Relationships: Is a person kind or cruel? A character may be capable of cruelty, but if they care for someone they may well want to avoid being hurtful to them. So, just as no character is a complete stereotype, so no person has the same relationship with everyone around them.

Relationships have a history, they affect the choices and actions that a character makes; they affect their emotions. If a relationship changes then the behavior of those involved will change. Many stories focus on how events challenge and change relationships.

In *The Reader*, the young man, Peter Berg, is shocked to see the woman he loves on trial, and this past relationship makes it hard for him to completely condemn her. Their former relationship determines his reactions, while the other characters in the story, those who have no former knowledge of the accused woman, are free to judge and despise her.

Conflict: A story is about a conflict. A person wants something and they have to face some sort of challenge or obstacle to get it. It could be the conflict of an epic journey or the conflict between two people in a room.

The essence of conflict and how it plays out in a story is underwritten by a character's super-objective, but defined by their relationship to what they struggle against; nature, society, people. Understanding the conflicts for each character in the story and the pinpointing of how a character relates to this challenge at each point of the narrative creates a line of actions and reactions the writer can trace out and follow through.

In the Edith Wharton's *Age of Innocence*, set within the fastidious strictures of the rule-bound high society of New York in the 1800's, a man wants to support a woman's reputation, and there is a conflict between the man and the society. This conflict is greatly increased when he and the woman fall in love, because this new circumstance can only end up in destroying both of them if it becomes public. Here the conflict is between the couple keeping their relationship secret, or saving their reputations by breaking off their love affair.

Tension: Conflicts and struggles create tension. The goals of the characters needs to be clear, what they want needs to be clear and the struggle and challenge they face needs to be clear. This does not mean that all characters in stories are highly motivated so they act decisively, or that the reader will fully understand everything about a character from the very start of a story, it means that the character is written with a clear and coherent set of personality traits. Tension comes when people interact, but they want different things. Without clear motivations and conflicts there is no tension in a story.

Beats: narrative beats and character beats
One method that is used to analyze the individual elements of a story is the idea of *beats*. This is an approach that is used mainly in film and drama directing, but it can also be usefully applied to novel writing.

The two types of beats are *narrative beats* and *character beats*. There are also *changes of beats*.

The idea behind each type of beat is relatively simple, which is why they are useful and practical as tools for breaking down a story and clarifying its constituent parts:

A narrative beat: a specific narrative event, the action of a story. Narrative beats will include all the plot points of the story, but they are precise in terms of action/event rather than being an outline of what happens.

A character beat: the motivation of a character that underpins a specific action or reaction. Character beats are more complex than story beats as each character involved in a story event has their own character beat.

A change of beats: an event where there is a conflict or change that takes the events of a story in a specific direction. A change of beats marks the end of a series of beats and represents the turning point of the scene or chapter.

In *The Great Gatsby*, the narrator, Nick Carraway, is attracted to the sportswoman, Jordan Baker. There is a *narrative beat* that changes this. Jordan lies about an incident with a car. The *character beat* that follows is that Nick is disillusioned with Jordan, and their developing relationship dissipates. This shift, from a growing attachment to an emotional break, is caused by a narrative event, which is a *change of beats*. It might have been possible for the story to be written so that Nick didn't care that Jordan lied, and he still wanted to be with her regardless of her morality, but this would go against Nick Carraway's character, and his sense of right and wrong.

When thinking about what to include in a story, a writer needs to understand what is vital. The incident with the car in *The Great Gatsby* is not a world shattering, action-packed event, but it is important to the story, because it leads to Carraway's disillusionment with people, which is the major theme of the novel.

In the planning a book, the author may well just want to get the events on the page as these come from the imagination. This is fine, but at a later stage considering the narrative beats and character beats can be very useful. A critical examination will help the author understand what their story is saying; how it will be understood by the reader. The use of beats to analyze a story allows a writer to refine and improve what they have written.

Please note: In relation to directing drama and film the term *beat* is also used to suggest a pause. In a film or play both the dialogue and action has a sense of rhythm and pace, and this rhythm can be stopped, paused for a moment – a beat. This is a musical idea of a beat: *narrative beats* and *character beats* are not beats in the sense of a rhythm.

Storytelling Terminology: You cannot use technical terms to create a story. Deciding that you want a climax, reversals, and things like character arcs and scene objectives, gives you no actual plot or events. But the use of terminology does become useful and relevant once a story is being refined.

You can learn to use storytelling terminology to test your story, and you will find that as you gain experience as a writer this terminology will help you decide on story events as you create them. You will begin to imagine stories and want them to have clear narrative beats, you will know how to use unseen action, and suspense.

The first stage in using terminology is to develop an understanding of these terms by considering them in relation to pre-existing novels, and seeing how you can understand and analyze these stories. Once you can do this, then you can apply the terminology to your own writing.

Storytelling: Mythic, Social, Psychological

There are many recognized types of story in terms of style and genre: satire, parody, grotesque, absurd, comedy-drama, tragic-comedy, black comedy, etc.. You might want to write a particular style of novel, and follow this as a guide, but you might also want to consider your story in relation to the following broader terms: Mythic, Social, Psychological.

Mythic Storytelling

Mythic stories are idealistic, heroic, fairytale, wish fulfillment. They carry social metaphors, allegory, 'universal stories', 'timeless' drama. These stories, even if they appear to be set in a specific social setting, are in fact highly idealized and they work to simplify and correct the problems and complexities of the real world. To do this they use plots and characters within a simplistically defined realism.

Mythic stories have:

Good vs. Evil: A defined moral structure. A world in which there is justice and injustice, and justice prevails.

Archetypal roles: Heroes and villains, innocents and monsters, incorruptible cops and criminal masterminds. There can be characters with super powers, special gifts, and these characters, whether actual super-heroes with super powers, or just heroic individuals who are brave and fearless, all have the ability to survive hardships and punishment without suffering the long-term physical or psychological damage that real people would. They are heroes in the mythic world, even if a large element of world is jaded: Batman and Philip Marlowe.

Mainstream genre fiction: Mythic stories have popular mass appeal. They are works of mainstream fiction. They offer broadcast codes. Epic drama, they are thrillers, action and adventure, horrors, romance.

Plotting: In the mythic drama the story is plot driven. There are happy endings and heroic sacrifice is not in vain. The villain dies. The crime is solved. True love is found. Justice is served.

Characters know themselves: What a character is on the surface is the same as they are on the inside. External conflicts are between people on opposing sides, there are no complex social conflicts or inner psychological complexities. A hero may have some ethical doubts, a scarred past, a flaw to overcome, a sacrifice to make, but in the end they do the right thing.

Examples: The mythic drama includes any crime, action, or thriller, where the hero defeats the villain and good triumphs over evil. For example the James Bond novels of Ian Fleming and any number of fictional detectives: Poirot, Marlowe and Harry Bosch. Also, the comic book heroes of childhood, and the contemporary heroes, created by authors such a Lee Child, Patricia Cornwall, Dan Brown and Tom Clancy. Above all else, no matter how gritty and realistic these stories appear to be, they are about wish fulfillment and things turn out well at the end. The hero is indestructible.

In a heroic mythic, fantasy world, Harry Potter survives death and the evil of Lord Voldermort is punished. In a seemingly real military world, the US army, which is actually still mythic, Jack Reacher finds the bad guys, he fights them and survives; nothing can stop Jack Reacher. He's as heroic, brave and fearless as any comic book hero.

What myth does is idealize the hero and create a sense that the individual who fights for their beliefs has integrity and that society benefits because of this. This is why these stories are 'timeless' and 'universal' and why they can cross national boundaries; the idea of a hero who gives up their own selfish aims to be of services to defeat evil is important to any society; because every society expects some degree of self-sacrifice; to protect it, to make it strong.

Social Storytelling

Social stories represent and mediate the values of a society; its norms, and its morals. To identify examples of this type story of one looks for writers who are seen as having a strong social perspective. Classic social writers are Edith Wharton, Henry James, John Steinbeck, Ernest Hemmingway, Gustave Flaubert, Guy de Maupassant. Social novels don't have to be serious. They can be comic as in Charles Dickens, because exaggerations point out social roles, etiquettes and social boundaries.

Social storytelling is about responsibilities, institutions, individual identity versus social identities: the tensions and dilemmas within society. Here you can't have a hero step in and solve the problem because that would not be realistic; in this context presenting a heroic solution would be a plot trick and a false way out, because social stories are bound to the realities of the society.

Social stories feature:

Institutions: Social storytelling takes place within recognizable social environments. They are legal stories, police stories, political stories, family stories. Social stories can have a contemporary or a historical setting. When a story is set in the past this social world offers a comparison to contemporary morals.

Good vs. Evil: As with mythic realism, social stories offer a moral universe that, more often than not, punishes the wrong and brings the world to good order. There is plenty of wish fulfillment, because a society, in the end needs to be shown to be fair and just, and to support and protect the honest and decent individuals who live within it.

Social stories are: primarily plot driven, but underpinned by consistency of character. Characters have back-stories which clearly create their social identity, beliefs and morals. Conflicts are external or interpersonal. Characters are usually understandable and consistent in their behavior and actions. Character can change and develop, character is not fixed as it is with archetypal heroes and villains, but they remain clearly defined. Characters have understandable motivations.

Psychological Storytelling: Intimate Realism

When stories shift from the mythic and social and move much closer to the individual, then they can become internal and psychological. With intimate realism identity and reality is contradictory, complex. The idea of a coherent and rational social identity and individuality is diffuse and perhaps entirely lost. Characters don't easily fit into social identities, or feel displaced from society; *The Outsider, The Piano Teacher, Our Lady of The Flowers.*

In a story of intimate realism:

Characters: veer between apparent free will and compulsion in their actions and motivations. Inner conflicts and motivations seem to underpin and determine action, but the reasons why characters act as they do is not openly apparent. Characters do not know themselves. They cannot justify their motivations through any accepted moral norm.

Morality is uncertain: Characters can be understood as immoral, amoral or even unmoral in relation to social norms. (Unmoral; because there is no clear moral universe by which to judge their actions) Social norms can be oppressive, contradictory, but are also often diffuse, indeterminate, even absent.

Motivations: stem from inner psychological conflict. Characters may have specific social roles, but that does not define who they are.

Narrow cast: These stories do not offer social or moral role models. They are narrowcast. Stories are character driven. These stories might be labeled extreme, inexplicable, irrational, even perverse. Natsuo Karino is labeled a crime writer, but her novels *Out, Real Girls* and in particular *Grotesque*, are studies of the psyche; plot is sacrificed or reduced in favor of inner monologue. There is no good guy who wins, just those who become involved in crime.

Myth, Social Realism, and Intimate Realism
If these three outlines, descriptions of stories in terms of mythic realism, social storytelling and psychological realism seem too broad to be useful then be sure that you understand and set out clearly the specific rules for realism for your own stories. Each story constructs its own reality and this needs to be coherent within the framework of the novel.

Storytelling technique: Comic writing
The simplest way of looking at comedy is to say that it surprises, startles, shock or delights us and the essential aspect of all comedy is that it goes beyond the ordinary, the dull and the familiar. If a man

goes into a bakery and comes out with a loaf of bread, that is not funny. If a man goes into a bakery and struggles out the door with a loaf of bread that's the size of a washing machine that has the potential to be funny because it can be a comic exaggeration. Comedy pushes the barriers of behavior, and goes beyond the reader's anticipation of what someone is going to say or do.

To achieve this heightened reality comedy uses a whole range of comic tactics from absurdity to mockery, to sarcasm to irony. The whole impetus of comedy is to create a distance, a perspective on the world, a world that is no longer pedestrian, but comic. Each of the tactics of comedy disturbs, disrupts, alters and changes things from what is expected. Comedy plays with the world, changing it, distorting it, and in doing so creates, the glee, the relief and the enjoyment of laughter. To write comedy one has to put these comic tactics to good use and the first step toward this is to understand the range of approaches that are available to the writer, rather than just trying to be comic using an unspecific idea of what might be funny.

It is a popular myth that comedy is much more difficult to create than drama; that it's too hard to understand and explain how comedy works and therefore much harder to write it. This situation may have come about from a combination of reasons. Firstly, comedy is not a single entity, so trying to understand comedy as a single sort of emotional experience is not practical. This means that many people only have a vague idea of what 'comedy' is in relation to analyzing and understanding it; we laugh, but we don't really know why. And what follows on naturally from this vagueness is the second problem that when people want to write comedy they don't really know what they are after. Given this vagueness, making a definite distinction between real life and comedy needs to be clearly drawn in order to help comic writing.

In life social behavior is more often than not limited by self-restraint and in terms of one person's relationship with another a single off hand cutting remark that says what *you really think of someone* can end in long-term animosity.

In comedy restraint is given up and what's usually left unspoken is said. In comedy the conceit is that comments can fly, behavior can be flagrantly hurtful, but no one takes long-term offence.

In life the excesses of pride, arrogance, selfishness, defiant stupidity, dumb naivety and salacious desire are likely to leave you ostracized, ignored or detested.

In comedy it's the display of pride, arrogance, selfishness, defiant stupidity, dumb naivety and salacious desire that's funny. In comedy a character gets to be who they *really are*; greedy, sexist, bullying, and if they suffer because they have these awful qualities, then that's funny as well.

In life we regret, possibly even dread, the revelation of our weaknesses, flaws and failures, because of the shame and anxiety they cause us.

In comedy failures, flaws and weaknesses can't be concealed. They're in the open and the reader laughs; sometimes with a sense of embarrassment, because they feel worries about their own flaws being uncovered, and then sometimes it's a laugh of relief, because the reader's own failures aren't nearly so awful in comparison to the exaggerations of comedy fiction.

In life, each day, there are a few minor problems, perhaps one or two funny moments and we get by without too many mishaps or making too much of a fool of ourselves.

In comedy a minor problems soon escalates and reaches new heights in terms of complexity and the potential for failure or embarrassment become huge. The reader laughs because their own lives aren't so bad, and in comedy it's only pretend. In life, real problems offer no such comic distance.

In life there are a few people who exhibit extremes, but most people, most of the time, are reasonable and reasonably reserved.

In comedy characters are sharply drawn. A character who is dumb keeps being dumb. A worrier will worry endlessly about everything. Even a dull ordinary person is extremely grey and extremely dull.

In life lying, plotting, scheming, hiding and denying are to be concealed, because they make people distrust you and can socially stigmatize you. In life, if you're caught out, then you might not be able to laugh it off, because you've hurt and betrayed someone

In comedy the anxiety of lying, trying to hide something, the machinations, the lengths someone will go to in order hold aloft a false front and conceal the truth are all part of the fun and games. There's laughter in seeing the effort to conceal and in seeing someone fail to conceal.

In life it's rude to laugh at someone when they show their flaws and failing.

In comedy the reader is invited to laugh and openly enjoy the flaws, ineptitude and crassness of the characters. When a reader enjoys a comedy laughter is a two-sided joy. The reader can laugh *at a character* because the character's behavior is so socially flagrant or inept or inappropriate. The reader can also laugh in sympathy *with a character* because they can empathize with that failure, flaw or faux pas.

Categories of Comedy

In life there is the normal, the boring, the everyday, the common, the dull, the serious while comedy undermines, ridicules, mocks, observes and comments on these. Comedy is having fun and the most common term to describe what is needed for a comedy approach is **comic distance**; a perspective on the world that makes it funny. These are different comic attitudes:

Stupid Comedy Those who are bungling, unskilled, and can't cope with the world, or those who are made to feel inferior by others, don't give up and hide in shame, but proudly play by their own rules and the normal world suffers as a result. The stupid make the proud and serious suffer.

Clever Comedy Taking a knowing look at the world, dissecting its foibles, pointing out its idiocies, making fun of what traps and demeans others. Clever comedy makes things more bearable and makes people laugh because they can view the world from a critical, often ironic, distance.

Social Comedy We live within social norms. There's an etiquette and a social standard for everything. In the social comedy people's desires are greater, their problems exaggerated. Seeing all the intricacies, rules, and our own standards of behavior highlighted, pushed to the limit, and even broken gives us the distance we need for comedy.

Comedy of absurdity The real world has failed so something replaces it, but of course people are still people and things still go wrong. Each absurdity is a metaphor or exaggeration of a world that is familiar to us.

Comedy of Delight What if all the obstacles were removed, and all the venality and cruelty were banished. That's when the world becomes wonderful and laughter is joyful and a sign of delight and pleasure.

With these approaches to comedy it is possible to move on from this is to understand which elements of comedy fit inside them. The world of the stupid comedy contains, crudity, embarrassment, silliness and of course stupidity, while the clever comedy has the epigrams, the aphorisms, the wit and the knowing innuendo. The comedy of absurdity has the hyperbole, the fantastic, the absurd, while comic delight is filled with whimsy, synchronicity, and of course the delightful. It possible to identify comic techniques, types of joke, and with these tools a writer can really be sure of what type of joke they are aiming for. Here's an alphabetical list:

Absurdity The ridiculous and the nonsensical. The real world transformed into the fantastic; the absurd leading to a world of wonder, or even to the opposite, a world where things are worse than ever.

Aphorism A clever witticism where a clever social observation is seen as apt or acute

Coincidence When the disaster that's been likely to happen wreaks havoc, the laughter begins. When events transpire to bring out hidden secrets then the reader joins in the fun.

Crudity When the polite world is disrupted or has to confront sex and other bodily functions, there is laughter in embarrassment and recognition

Delight When that wonderful thing occurs, followed by another wonderful thing and as this keeps going a smile of wonder can turn to a laugh of delight

Embarrassment It is humorous when others lose their dignity without regret when for us the same situation would be one we dread.

Epigram A clever remark for a knowing laugh

Euphemism Politely referring to something that is unpleasant or embarrassing, while making sure that what's rude is plainly understood.

Exaggeration Each of us has our small troubles, but to see them magnified allows us the release of laughter. To see the foibles and failings of the world, its pretensions and petty vanities, and to exaggerate them, is to make them comical.

Hyperbole An extravagant exaggeration that pokes fun at the normal world

Innuendo To insult, to demean, to sexualize: when the hidden meaning is salacious, but the words are innocent, is to carry on a covert and amusing conversation.

Irony To say exactly the opposite of what you are actually implying, makes it clear exactly what you mean. It's an attack with a humorous distance

Demean The proud, the vain, the self-important; it's fun to see those who want to lord it over us demeaned and ridiculed

Literalism Something is said; we know its colloquial meaning, but it's literal meaning makes something else, something unexpected happen.

Mockery To ridicule the pretensions, rules and traditions that you are surrounded by is to poke fun at the world

One-upmanship When someone wants to put you down its fun to get the better of them and let everyone know it

Punning Phrases and words have more than one meaning. A pun can just be a silly comparison or a pointed re-working of a popular phrase, or saying.

Rudeness To be impolite and offensive is to refuse respect, and to challenge customs and taboos. To mock and ridicule the conventional is a comic weapon.

Sarcasm Insincerity is the easiest defense to all trials and tribulations

Sauciness Suggesting that sex is naughty, but fun, can raise a knowing smile

Silliness Why takes thing seriously? Make the pompous trivial, the serious silly.

Stupidity To refuse or to be unable to cope with the world, to refuse to cope with the world is to undermine its norms.

Synchronicity The incredible, the wondrous, makes the world less drab and less grey. There is an escape from the dull and familiar, it can and does happen

Understatement To make light of the serious, to refuse to be afraid or unimpressed is to take a comic distance.

Whimsy To link something serious to something you find odd of fanciful. It makes the world a funnier place.

Wordplay To play with language, to twist its meaning, its sounds, its everyday use is to have fun.

First and Second Narrative
The serious, sensible story, the drama, the tragedy, the epic, is one kind of narrative describing our existence. Comedy adds a second narrative: it comments on the world and distorts it. The reader, the audience enjoys comedy, because it is a step away from reality. Hamlet can be a tragic character, but in a comedy he's a simpering, self-centered whiner. Comedy shows us that problems and failures, and life itself, can been seen from a distance as odd and absurd: people try to be serious and sensible, but they can't keep up this performance forever.

Writing Technique

The Writing Style of Contemporary Popular Fiction

If you want to write a novel using the contemporary style for popular fiction these are the guidelines to follow.

Set out below are sections dealing with the types of sentences needed to tell a story in a novel, the construction of sentences and paragraphs, the choice of vocabulary, the use of viewpoint, the use of time, temporality, and the writing of dialogue. This is the style of writing you will find in the mainstream novels of today; the books on the best seller lists. While there are many styles of writing and different approaches to storytelling that can be used for the novel this is the one that is dominant.

The story of a novel is told using four different types of sentence:

> Immediate action
> Summary action
> Description
> Commentary

The passage below is written in the style of contemporary popular fiction and makes use of these four different types of sentence. It is written in imitation of a mainstream detective story.

> *Using the address he had written down Jack left the squad room and drove to Pasadena using the freeway. It took him about an hour.*
>
> *The rundown motel rooms sat in a squat line with a double parking bay in front of each room. Five cars were parked; empty and still. Outside of number six was the pick-up with the dented rear-side door. Jack parked, pulling in alongside the dusty pick-up.*
>
> *Climbing out of his car, walking to the motel door Jack reached out to knock. He paused, his hand forming into a tight fist. He steadied himself, straightened his spine and he took a long deep breath. He knocked loudly; a hard triple tap.*
>
> *Jack had paused before knocking because when the door opened he knew he had to be ready. He'd see a middle-aged man with a puzzled expression. They would talk: Jack asking questions until there were too many lies to continue without the man reaching for an obvious, faltering falsehood. This tactic was the only way to win. Going in heavy-handed wouldn't get any sort of result. Jack's opponent was too clever, too wary to be surprised by this early*

> *morning visit. It had taken so long to reach this moment that there was no need to hurry.*

In the passage on the previous page the first paragraph is **summary action**:

> *Using the address he had written down Jack left the squad room and drove to Pasadena using the freeway. It took him about an hour.*

Summary action recounts events without detail, jumping over periods of time. It keeps the story, the action and the locations clear, but it is skimming over events, where the detail of what is happening is relatively uninvolving or unimportant to the through-line of the story.

The good thing about summary action is precisely because it provides a way of moving the story along quickly and clearly without getting bogged down in unnecessary detail and description. However, lengthy passages of summary action will become distant and unemotional for the reader. A news headline might summarize, *three people killed in road accident,* but if this event is to have emotional impact it is best to tell it with immediate action so that it is directly experienced by the reader.

These three sentences are **description**:

> *The rundown motel rooms sat in a squat line with a double parking bay in front of each room. Five cars were parked; empty and still. Outside of number six was the pick-up with the dented rear-side door.*

Descriptive sentences describe the setting of the story in terms of time and place, and description also sets outs the appearance of the characters and the way they dress.

In classic literary fiction, before the advent of photography, film and television, the author would describe the setting with a fairly large amount of detail. It was necessary to give this level of description, often metaphorically, because it helped the reader to imagine the setting of the story.

In contemporary fiction the need for description is much less. From the descriptive sentences used in the paragraph above the modern reader can imagine the setting of a *rundown motel,* they don't need a lot of detailed description because they have a much more developed vocabulary of images: they've seen motels in films, on TV, in photographs. Even if they haven't seen a motel they will be familiar with images of rather featureless, commodity-style, unremarkable buildings.

Because English Literature is always taught in schools with Classic Literature as its base it is often presumed by new writers that detailed descriptive and figurative writing is better writing than spare, sparse writing; this is not the case. Conventions in the novel, between Classic and contemporary fiction have changed and a story can start to feel sluggish if it has too much description. It can also feel verbose and artificial. Just as the style of speech has changed over the last two hundred years, so has the style of writing.

If an author, writing in the contemporary style, gives a long detailed description it should be because it is essential to the story, otherwise the description should be minimal so it doesn't crowd out and slow down the immediate action. Sometimes this is a difficult discipline for a new author to follow. Most new writers have to control their inclination to overwrite – they write a story as they see it and end up providing far too much detail. A popular novel needs only essential description: no more. The reader can add their own embellishments; the readers supply their own images for the story.

These three sentences are **immediate action**:

Climbing out of his car, walking to the motel door Jack reached out to knock. He paused, his hand forming into a tight fist. He steadied himself, straightened his spine and he took a long deep breath. He knocked loudly; a hard triple tap.

Immediate action is what is happening in the moment, as if in real time: the characters are doing something; it's happening now. Immediate action is the most important element of the popular fiction novel. The writer takes the reader on a journey following the main characters, often just one central character, taking their viewpoint as the story takes place; experiencing their actions.

As the term suggests what you get from immediate action is *immediacy*. You need immediate action to have a story that feels as if it is being lived out. It's the physicality, the *doing* of the story that's keeps the story moving, not the thinking of the characters, not the description of the setting or the appearance of the people in the story.

Successful, popular authors are highly proficient at writing immediate action, while neophyte authors often bog down their stories with passive writing, metaphorical and symbolic description and a point-by-point analysis of the characters' thoughts and decisions. The professional writer will imagine far more about each event in the story than they actually put down on the page, but rather than being long-winded, and including everything possible about each event in the story, they write with concision and clarity, staying with the flow of empathy which is created using immediate action.

This paragraph is **commentary:**

> Jack had paused before knocking because when the door opened he knew he had to be ready. He'd see a middle-aged man with a puzzled expression. They would talk: Jack asking questions until there were too many lies to continue without the man reaching for an obvious, faltering falsehood. This tactic was the only way to win. Going in heavy-handed wouldn't get any sort of result. Jack's opponent was too clever, too wary to be surprised by this early morning visit. It had taken so long to reach this moment that there was no need to hurry.

Commentary comes from the viewpoint of a character or from the omniscient narrator. With commentary the author is giving ideas directly to the reader. In this example it is the thoughts of the character that are used to provide commentary – Jack is explaining to himself, and to the reader, what they think is going to happen – it is not summarizing action and it is not immediate action – it is commentary presented as thought.

Commentary allows for a recap of the story, the inclusion of thoughts and musings. This appears to add depth and significant meaning to a story, but if it is overused commentary brings things to a standstill, because nothing is actually happening; the events aren't moving forward. It's like the coach talking to the team players when the game is paused. Commentary is an overview; it's not immediate and it's not in the moment. Commentary also pre-empts the reader's own interpretation of the story, so it can feel condescending to read a story where the author is always telling the reader what to think of a situation and how to react.

Sentences and Paragraphs

If you open the pages of a piece of classic fiction, such as Joesph Conrad, Henry James or Gustave Flaubert, and then compare it to a contemporary popular novel, John Grisham, Dan Brown or Lee Child, one thing that is distinct is the difference in the size of the paragraphs and more often than not the length of the sentences. In the contemporary novel, the sentences are simple, comprising one or two short clauses. Classic fiction will have simple sentences, but it will also use complex sentences with multiple clauses.

In modern popular fiction it is not uncommon to find a paragraph that is a short single sentence and the functionality of this style of writing controls the length of a paragraph: each sentence and paragraph says what it needs to say and then moves on.

For instance, in the example at the start of this section, the arrival of Jack at the motel, which is written in the style of a contemporary novel, there is a summary paragraph, a descriptive paragraph, a paragraph with immediate action and a paragraph of commentary. They are clear and distinct. Classic fiction, with its long paragraphs might mix description, commentary, action and even dialogue into extensive, ambling paragraphs. The writing technique of the contemporary novel stems more from the short-form pragmatic writing style of journalism than it does from the classic novel.

Vocabulary

Since the aim of the popular novel is to be readable to a majority of readers it uses a very clear, simple, everyday vocabulary. One way of deciding on the range of this vocabulary is to limit it to the vocabulary of the main characters or the setting of the story. Thus, a story about an LA cop or a Miami reporter, or a UK detective, will be defined by the types of words they would use. Taking this approach to vocabulary has the advantage of adding realism to a story; the vocabulary will feel authentic because it matches the environment. If, instead a writer chooses to step beyond the range of the characters, then the viewpoint of the story will change, and the reader will sense the presences of the writer commentating on the people and events in the story.

Keeping to this rule; the idea of using a vocabulary suitable for the characters or the setting; if a story is set in the past it will, in order to appear authentic, make use of a vocabulary suitable to that period and probably one based on classic fiction. If a story is set in the future or in an alternate world then this is likely to have a very specific vocabulary so that it does not appear too prosaic and contemporary. The fictional worlds of the future foreground the use of words based on technology and science. Futuristic novels may use neologisms; coining their own words.

Actual contemporary vocabulary, the words people speak and write in life, are changing and the present tendency is to incorporate computer, technology, science, sociology and medical terminology into everyday use and many words are becoming abbreviated. This will as a matter of course influence the vocabulary of novels placed in a contemporary setting. However, in terms of writing style, popular fiction does not write in the vernacular. It does not use, to any great extent, the words, phrasings or idioms of any particular class, social or ethnic group. The vernacular is avoided because it would severely limit who could read the novel and who it would appeal to. When considering an international reader for a book there can also be the issue of translation: a clear writing style with a fairly standard vocabulary is relatively straightforward to translate, which is what allows a novel to travel across languages, and what appeals to publishers when they are looking to publish popular fiction

Viewpoint

Many contemporary novels stay with a single character throughout the whole story, so that every chapter in the book is written from their viewpoint, telling their actions and depicting their experiences as events progress.

This approach to the story can be written in the third person viewpoint, but favoring a specific central character:

> *Using the address he had written down Jack left the squad room and drove to Pasadena using the freeway. It took him about an hour.*

It is clear that *Jack* is the character who is being favored even though the third person is being used. No one else's viewpoint is given.

In terms of using third person point of view, the contemporary style is not omniscient. It does not treat characters equally; only one specific character's viewpoint is privileged and everyone else is seen from that viewpoint. There is no sense that there is an overarching narrator commentating sympathetically or ironically on the events of the story.

When a story follows a single character through every chapter it can obviously be written in first person throughout, because, by definition, the story is told through one central character. In this case Jack becomes 'I'.

> *Using the address I had written down I left the squad room and drove to Pasadena using the freeway. It took me about an hour.*

First person viewpoint places certain strains on the writer, and this is because if it is strictly held then everything should be told from a single subjective experience. In the paragraph below the frequent use of 'I'; *I paused, I knew, I had, I'd see, I would, I saw*, would, across the length of long novel become over-repetitive and grate with the reader.

I paused before knocking because when the door opened I knew I had to be ready. I'd see a middle-aged man with a puzzled expression. I would talk to him. I would be the one asking the questions, watching, waiting, until I saw the lie that let me know that the man couldn't continue without reaching for an obvious, faltering falsehood. I had to be ready

This problem, of being stuck with the overuse of 'I' in a first person novel, and also of having to say what 'I' sees or looks at, in order to establish setting and surroundings, is overcome with something of a slight of hand in terms of using viewpoint. The first person takes a single character's viewpoint, but other people, places and things can be described as if from a third person point of view. This subtlety split use of the first persons means that the author does not have to keep using; *I saw, I looked, I noticed,* over and over again. Here is the paragraph from above re-written, still using a first person perspective, but incorporating 'third-person' commentary and description.

I paused before knocking because when the door opened I knew I had to be ready. A middle-aged man with a puzzled expression would answer. He would talk, answering questions until he reached the point where he couldn't continue without reaching for a faltering falsehood, a lie. He would be trapped and I would have him.

The first person point of view by definition places the reader with a single character, but the contemporary style allows the subtle use of the third person, to give scope for description. However, this style will not jump to the internal thoughts of a secondary character. The reader stays with the protagonist, inside them, with their personal viewpoint and not with any other person in the story.

If, instead of a single viewpoint, a writer wanted to tell a story from the viewpoint of several characters within a scene, then the writer would have to use omniscient third person, which would allow them to dip into the minds, thoughts and experiences of several characters. However, the author isn't likely to give the internal thoughts of every character at every event point the story.

In the Harry Potter novels, Harry Potter's internal thoughts and emotions are presented to the reader, and so to some extents are those of his friends; Hermione and Ron. These are the young people in the story. What is not given, is the internal life of the adults. These books are for young readers and the viewpoint is from the point of view of the young characters. The author J.K. Rowling structures the story and controls the viewpoint for her preferred reader.

In terms of the psychological reality used in first person novels both emotion and thought are represented pragmatically, not at a complex psychological level or as a representation of actual thinking. The contemporary popular fiction style does not use stream of consciousness.

Viewpoint can seem like a technical issue, because it sets rules for writing, but it is an issue, perhaps most of all, about how the author wants to tell the story and present the characters. The effect created by the careful control of third person viewpoint can be seen in *Chasing the Dime*, by Michael Connelly. Here the novel's viewpoint is used to articulate an important theme and also crucial plot elements of the story.

Chasing the Dime, a crime novel, has Henry Pierce as the central character. The story tells all the events from Henry's viewpoint using the third person. There are no scenes or chapters where Henry is not present. His feelings, particularly his feelings for his former wife are given to the reader. However, there is also something of a leakage of the truth in the third person style regarding Henry's relationship with his wife. Henry is not entirely honest in his understanding of himself; his account of his behavior towards his wife is not consistent. He remembers events and thinks he was loving husband, but there is definite a sense that he was not so doting and, also, there is a hint that he has harassed, perhaps even stalked his ex-wife.

Henry's internal life, (controlled by Michael Connelly's use of viewpoint) is not totally reliable and this presentation of Henry as somewhat misguided and obsessive links thematically with his wish to track down a missing woman who he has never seen or met. The search for the woman is justified by the reader's understanding of Henry's internal life; his obsessive nature, and this sense of the central protagonist's character, supports a major plotline of the novel.

Later in the story Henry is himself suspected of murdering this missing woman and this is justified, because the reader can see how other characters in the story view Henry and why they doubt and question his actions and motives. The third person viewpoint gives Henry's internal view of events, an external view of events and the contradictions between these two link to support the character motivation, plotting and theme for the novel.

The climax of *Chasing the Dime* uses a manipulation of plotting based on viewpoint.

Up until the ending of the novel Henry and the reader have been implicitly and inseparably linked together. For over two hundred pages whatever Henry does the reader is with Henry and follows his actions. However, to catch the murderer and to make this a surprise for the reader, Henry sets up a trap to catch the killer, but, crucially, this happens without the reader learning of these events – it is unseen action.

In this climactic chapter, and for the only time in the novel, Henry does things that are highly significant to the story which the reader is not aware of. The rules of viewpoint are changed to misdirect the reader: they believe that Henry is trapped and helpless when in fact this is part of pre-arranged plan to prove he is innocent.

The sudden and single manipulation of viewpoint in *Chasing the Dime* is very specific and it would be a mistake to change the rules of viewpoint again and again as a novel progresses. If Henry kept doing things that the reader did not see the novel would have shifted away from the consistency and *truthfulness* of viewpoint expected for popular fiction.

Changing viewpoints in a novel

If viewpoint changes within a popular novel it is only going to change from chapter to chapter, not within chapters, and it is only done so the story can move between major protagonists: chapters with the hero and chapters with the villain. The popular novel does not use multiple viewpoints from a wide range of characters and the popular novel would only very rarely, almost never, confuse viewpoints within a chapter. It is always completely clear in a popular novel which character's point of view is being given whether it is the first or the third person.

The Narrows, a crime novel, written by Michael Connelly, changes character viewpoint for different chapters.

There are chapters with Harry Bosch, the detective as the featured character and they are written in the first person. He is the central character of a set of novels written by Connelly, and in *The Narrows*, Harry Bosch's first person status makes clear his central significance to the story. Rachel Walling is an FBI agent. Her story is followed in a number of chapters and these are written from the third person viewpoint. The serial killer who is being hunted in the story, Richard Backus, has chapters following his actions; they are written in the third person. At the climax of the novel when all the major characters are together in the same chapter; then Harry Bosch is first person while Rachel Walling and Richard Backus remains in the third person. If each of the characters had been written in the first person the climactic chapters would have to use three first person viewpoints, which could only be confusing and the reader would find it almost impossible to follow which 'I' is doing what.

The switching of viewpoint in *The Narrows* is never confusing to the reader; it jumps between just the three main characters which is not difficult to follow. However, in *The Rules of Attraction*, Bret Easton Ellis, uses first person viewpoint with multiple characters, so there are many 'I's in the book. This is confusing and deliberately so. Viewpoint is used to present a range of ideas; the self-centeredness of contemporary adolescent life, society's impersonality and anonymity; its de-centered immorality. *The Rules of the Attraction* is deliberate, literary fiction; it aims for complexity, but the author of popular fiction aims for clarity, and doesn't use viewpoint to question or disrupt the sense of coherent and comprehensible reality.

Temporality: the use of time in popular fiction

The *Rules of Attraction* by Brett Easton Ellis, confuses viewpoints and it confuses time; the multiple first-person narrators recount their experience of events and these events overlap and repeat; a party takes place and different chapters, featuring different characters, return to the same point in time and as a consequence of these repeats and returns the story loses linearity; there is no clear beginning, middle and end. This is not the practice of popular fiction, which favors a clear linear progression; one event happens after another like a, b, c, with a story that goes from start to finish along a clear and coherent timeline.

When planning out the plot of a popular novel the author may well imagine a story taking place within a particular time span; a day, two days, a fortnight, a period of weeks. The story then sets out events along that timeline, which creates a temporal coherence for the reader; they sense the pace and timescale of the story even if it is not explicitly stated. (Some books even put explicit indicators of the time, or the date, as part of the headings for chapters, and this makes it absolutely clear when events are happening.)

Given that the reader is following a story as a flow of events, a linear progression of time, this poses two problems for the telling of a story. Firstly, explaining past events that effect the present, (how to reveal the back story in the main story) and secondly, overcoming jumps and unevenness in a story, where the writer wants to depict only the most dramatic events: this is the issue of how to move past incidents that would be long-winded, and uneventful to describe in full, although they are part of the timespan of the narrative.

The flashback is one way of returning to the past and a chapter or a number of chapters - a section in a novel - might recount earlier events.

In *Red Dragon* by Thomas Harris, three chapters are devoted to recounting the early life of the serial killer, Francis Dolarhyde. These chapters delay the linear progression of the novel, but they are not particularly disruptive as they give important information and they are discrete; three chapters in a fifty-four chapter novel. What would become disruptive was is if the novel jumped back and forth recounting the back stories of all the other characters. For instance, two other characters in *Red Dragon*, Will Graham, who is an FBI investigator and Hannibal Lecter, the serial killer, share a significant back story; Will Graham captured Lecter and Hannibal Lecter nearly killed Will Graham. In the book this back story is not told through flashback, but revealed through conversation, so that it is told very briefly and with no real detail concerning what happened.

Conversation, dialogue, people talking about the past, is a simple device for clarifying the back story. In *The Davinci Code* and *Angel and Demons*, written by Dan Brown, the main character, the symbologist Robert Langdon explains what has happened in the past which avoids any need for jumps back and forth in time.

As a rule, in the popular novel, multiple flashbacks are avoided and the past is usually revealed through conversation, or by commentary. This in effect keeps the story 'in the present' and the temporality linear. Jumping in time is likely to diminish immediacy and it is maintaining a sense of immediacy that is the first principal for a novel written in the dominant contemporary style.

There is difference here between cinematic storytelling and literary storytelling with films making more frequent use of flashbacks because these are more visually interesting than having someone on-screen talking about what has happened.

One device that is frequently used in novels to set out events in the past and provide a framework for the setting and the relationships in the story is the prologue. This is usually done in a single chapter at the very start of the book; telling a specific event and the story then jumps ahead in time and the main story commences. The prologue makes it unnecessary for the story to use flashbacks or to jump back in time at other stages in the story.

Prologues can also be used for flash forwards: the description of events that happen toward the end of the story as it is told in the main part of the book. The flash forward offers the promise of a dramatic ending to a story, without telling the events of in full, and the reader wants to follow the main story so that the route to get to this climax becomes clear to them.

If a story does need to have significant jumps in time; if there is a large break in the timeline of the story, then this can be controlled by having a book which is split into different parts. In *Grotesque* by Natsuo Kirino, the novel is in eight parts. The first part tells the story of the early life of the characters and the later parts jumps to when the characters are adult. This method, separate parts of the novel for different periods of time offers clear temporal breaks and ensures that the reader is not disturbed or confused from chapter to chapter.

The issue that underpins all of the problems regarding temporality is verisimilitude, which is the sense that the story is real and authentic, that it is *happening*. If a story jumps back and forth awkwardly in time, leaps and pauses in a haphazard way, has odd gaps in time, doesn't make it clear what is happening and when it is happening, then it becomes a jumble; it falls apart as a story and the reader senses that the narrative is a poorly constructed artifice. The writing style of popular fiction sets out ways to avoid a loss of verisimilitude. It main tenets are:

- Temporality is linear; a story is told from start to finish, without complexity in terms of time

Back story can be presented through:

- Prologues
- Conversation or commentary

Significant jumps in time are signaled through:

- Chapter breaks
- Section/Part Breaks

Above all else plotting is managed to create a clear temporality in order to have a story where the action builds to a climax. Much of the work of creating a story implicitly addresses the issue of keeping the sequence of events coherent; the rule is for the writer to be sure that the reader knows what is happening and when.

Dialogue
While this might seem too limited and simplistic, a character in a novel speaks because:

- They want to say something
- They want to ask a question
- They are responding to someone

While there can be aphorisms, wit and irony in dialogue, such as in the writing of Oscar Wilde, most dialogue is functional: one character informs or questions another, or a character responds to another character. If dialogue goes beyond this, then it can seem verbose, chatty or meandering, to the reader.

When a writer wants to create dialogue with a sense of character this relies not on additional dialogue, but on carefully phrased and worded statements to match such things as class, race, age and gender.

The personality of a character is established by their actions and how they are described in the book. What they say, can, more often than not, be understood from this characterization and what is happening in the story.

If a character, who is described as strong-willed, refuses a request to do something with a simple, 'no', then the reader understands this dialogue as a firm statement. However, if another character says 'no', but this might be a lie, or the character who is speaking is described in the book as hesitant and uncertain, then the reader will create their own inflection: the reader will understand this, 'no', as being spoken with a falter of uncertainty.

There is no need to depict hesitation in a book through a continuous use of ellipsis or hyphens:

> 'Pleas.... can I say... that... I'm not going to do what you wan...'

This use of punctuation, to try and depict the verbal delivery of the words only interrupts that reader, and if it is done time and again in novel becomes disruptive. When the character and situation are clear to the reader, then how words are said will be understood and interpreted by the reader.

For a writer dialogue has two main styles. With or without comment:

With comment:

> 'Can I have a minute of your time?' Jack said, earnestly, wanting to speak. He needed to make sure that he wasn't being misunderstood.

Or, without comment:

> 'Can I have a minute of your time?' Jack said.

Alternatively:

'Can I have a minute of your time?' said Jack.

Or even with no identification of the speaker:

'Can I have a minute of your time?'

Popular fiction can make use of both types of dialogue, with and without comment, but the choice will be quite specific. It will depend on the style of the novel, its genre, and may even be determined by the gender of its main characters.

The pared down, hardboiled novel, the male dominated story, may use little else but 'he said' or 'she said' and the dialogue will have no comment, and this approach is taken in order for characters to be perceived as functional, unemotional and pragmatic.

When dialogue is supported with comment it can make the characters appear more sensitive and more emotional; they have a more visible internal life and their feelings are given to the reader. This is recognizable within the romance novel where inner emotions and feelings are brought to the fore by the writer.

Once the style of dialogue has been decided for a set of characters in a novel, this will then remain the same for the entire novel. There won't be chapters were characters exhibit a change in their emotional range; by having the dialogue move from no comment to comment. This is because such a change would represent a change in character.

Since many novels have little or no comment to accompany the dialogue and they use the pared-down style, it is expected that the reader will supply their own interpretation in order to understand the tone in which the words are said, and also, what the character intended in terms meaning. This is true in a large number of novels for adults.

However, in popular novels, written for the younger reader, the dialogue may well use extensive comment. The author will offer this explanation, so that the intention and feelings of the characters who are speaking are clear. The younger reader is expected to need this additional guidance:

So, dialogue for the adult reader:

'Be quiet.'

And for the younger reader:

'Be quiet,' said Billy, in a hoarse whisper to his friend. Billy didn't want their hiding place to be found.

This is dialogue with detailed comment, and it is done to make sure that the identity of the speaker, and the intention of their statement is understood.

Popular Fiction and Literary Fiction

Popular fiction might be contrasted with literary fiction and it can be useful to identify the distinctions between these two different strands of writing.

Popular fiction is pragmatic. Its aim is to tell a story in the clearest, most accessible way, with the clearest and most accessible prose. The overarching aim of clarity determines the register and the vocabulary of this kind of novel and the writer makes sure that viewpoint is consistent and easy for the reader to follow.

The narratives of popular fiction have a central protagonist or a limited range of central characters who provide the viewpoint for the story.

In popular fiction a book's narrative is structured through the back story and story of the central characters. The story has clear character-based motivations and a coherent plot: Dan Brown writes popular fiction, Lee Child writes popular fiction, as do a host of other popular and successful authors.

Popular fiction deserves to be looked down upon when it becomes hackneyed; if the writer relies on worn out, over-familiar phrases, stereotypical characters and clichéd plotting. Well written popular fiction has a precision and clarity that infuses the story with immediacy and emotion and this quality of writing, even though it is accessible requires considerable ability in terms of writing skill and imagination. There is a tendency to presume that literary fiction is 'better' than popular fiction. Popular fiction has its own particular aims, its own integrity and a book can be well or badly written according to these aims.

The novels of the eighteenth and nineteenth century, which are now regarded as classics; Austen, Dickens, etc. are one strand of literary fiction. These works often bear some of the hallmarks of popular fiction; they tell accessible stories. However, their register is comparatively verbose, descriptive and arcane, compared to contemporary popular fiction.

Making a comparison of a novel by Joseph Conrad, who writes a great deal of description and even metaphysical commentary, to that of the pared-down modern novel, by an author like John Le Carré, would demonstrate a clear distinction between the classic and the contemporary style of writing. Here, it is not question of who is a better writer, or what is better writing; old or new. The situation is that if anyone wrote a novel in the style of Joesph Conrad today, it would only seem like a pastiche of an outdated style, because the approach taken in modern popular fiction has shifted away from extensive intrusive commentary.

As a rejection of classic literature many early twentieth century authors, most prominently Ernest Hemmingway, favored very direct simple prose. This type of writing is one basis for the style of present day popular fiction; these novels tell stories that avoid any sort of omniscient commentary or metaphysical musing. However, this style of writing is still considered to be literary fiction because of its historical place in the development of the novel at the first half of the 20th century.

Since the 1920's there has also been modernist and literary fiction and the ambitions of this kind of writing are quite different from that of popular fiction, classis literature or bare-bones Hemmingway-style literature. The modernist, post-modern, or literary author, can pursue a number of aims:

- To produce a literary work aims to use language to express a range of psychological and metaphysical states; to write subjectively and introspectively; to produce novels where the story is secondary to expressiveness of the language.

- To create a style of writing that equates to lived experience.

- Literary works can also be concerned with their own fiction; they are inter-textual, deconstructive and aware of their own fabrications and become meta-fictions. These are experimental modernist, or post-modernist works.

The qualities of a modern literary novel can also be recognized because of its intellectual, social, or political ambitions. The importance of the subject makes a book a literary work because it presents ideas or themes beyond that of a genre story: these novels want to reflect on society; intellectually and critically. The genre writing of popular fiction is allegorical and mythic rather than socially and historically specific.

The hardboiled detective stories written by Raymond Chandler and Dashiell Hammett inhabit a mythologized, an allegorically simplified, version of the cities of Los Angeles and San Francisco: The PI is good, and the villain is bad. Literary writing shies away from the clear dichotomies of heroes and villains.

Within the domain of literary studies there is a constant question: what is a novel? This can be asked because there are so many different types of story and approaches to style. When one begins to work with narratives that manipulate temporality and character, even language itself, then the question of 'what is a novel?' emerges.

In contrast to the intellectual interrogation of the history and complexity of the many forms of the novel, the everyday reader, the consumer, goes into a bookshop or browses on-line and after flipping a few pages knows that a work is popular fiction or literary fiction. In this light the question 'what is a novel?' becomes redundant and the popular writer can take a similar stance.

When planning to write a book, worrying about critical distinctions between popular and literary fiction is not very helpful. What is necessary is for the author to be able to define the specifics, in terms of the story, the structure, and the writing style, of the book they are going to write: it's use of viewpoint, vocabulary, temporality, and dialogue. The popular fiction author needs to be clear in terms of distinguishing what type of sentence they are working with in order to tell the story: immediate, summary, commentary or description.

Successful writing technique
Below are a number of suggestions that can underpin a successful approach to creative writing technique:

Punctuation and grammar: A writer needs to be sure that they can understand and use simple and complex sentences, passive and active tense, full stops, colons, semi-colons, dashes, italics, apostrophes, bracketing commas, listing commas, joining commas, in fact grammar and punctuation in general. It's a good idea for a writer to have their own ready-to-hand reference books for this subject so that they can check and refer to them because there will always be a need to confirm and check what has been written.

Clarity and Simplicity: Writing in clear simple sentences that say directly what is happening in the story is the aim of most authors. They avoid the continuous use of a commentating narrator/viewpoint who supplies aphorisms, erudite comments and philosophical musings. The contemporary popular writer lets the story carry the meaning, not the wordiness of the prose. Popular authors avoid using metaphors and symbols unless they are particularly pertinent to the setting of the story.

Poor writing shows, when an author relies on the use of idioms: 'quick on the draw', 'like a duck to water'. Idioms are common in spoken language; they are familiar phrases and save time in communicating an idea or offering a description. In fiction writing idioms become trite and are a slack use of language, and just because they are easily at hand does not make them a good choice of language: they are unoriginal.

New writers often slip into common errors; the use of too many adjectives and adverbs. The reader doesn't need to have a qualifier for every description and action: a 'book', does not need to be a 'heavy large book', and 'running' does not need to be 'fast furious exhausting running'. If the story is clear then the constant use of adverbs and adjectives are not necessary:

This level of description tells the story effectively:

> *Using all his energy to run the man caught the train.*

In the example below, the verbose level of description becomes somewhat silly, especially if this approach were extended to an entire book:

> *Using all his stored and determined energy, the forlorn, lonely, sad, struggling man, forlornly caught the slowly moving ancient, doddering, train.*

There will be times when a writer needs to establish the quality of an object or event, but once this is done there is no need to keep on adding to the writing with florid phrasing. It is not necessary because the reader is able to imagine the situation and events for themselves: the extra verbiage is over-embellishing.

Another problem for new writers to watch out for is the repetitious use of words and phrases:

Without repetition:

> *Seeing the train arriving, the man got ready. When it stopped he got on.*

With unnecessary repetition:

> *Seeing the train arriving, the man got ready to get on board the arriving train. When the train stopped, he got ready to get on board the stopped train.*

Because writing is done in a flow, it's quite easy to be repetitive, and end up using the same description or words, and this problem can be avoided in the first draft by being alert, or it can edited out at a later stage.

Summary action and immediate action: Summary action presents an overview of events while immediate action describes events taking place in the moment. A story told entirely as summary action will seem distanced and impersonal, because it does not connect the reader directly with the actions and thoughts of the characters. Summary action is useful for establishing situations and relationships quickly and easily, but should not dominate a novel.

Immediate action is the heart of the novel; it's where the reader gets involved in the story: they forget they are reading and live with the characters.

A writer should identify the most important events in the story of the novel they are planning, and ensure that this is vividly written as immediate action: this is their aim, because what the writer of popular fiction wants to present clearly, over and above any sense of literary style, is a sense of unfolding events that will allow the reader to participate in the action and the life of the characters.

Moving between summary and immediate action allows the writer to expand and contract events so that they can tell a clear story which remains under control in terms of the overall length of novel and the length of each chapter.

New writers often write very long, rambling novels with very long and then short chapters showing no control over length, and in doing so, tell a story that carries too much information about events that could easily be summarized. There's no need to have every event as immediate action as this is a ponderous and stodgy way to tell a story and results in a stodgy, over-long novel.

Vocabulary: For direct and emotional storytelling writers choose a vocabulary that is suitable for the setting and characters. This will make the story more authentic. If an author writes a novel using a vocabulary that distances the reader from the story this will make it less involving for the reader. However, an author should not write in the vernacular, unless they are clearly expert with the type of language and the specifics of the argot and idiom they want to reproduce.

The best way to suggest the vernacular is to use one or two relevant words in the descriptive passages and again one or two words or phrases in the dialogue spoken by the characters; this will convince the reader about the authenticity of the social setting and the social background of the characters, while at the same time keeping the writing clear and understandable to a wide range readership.

Register and style: A register is a specific and limited range of language used by an author when writing, and also the style and vocabulary used in life by a specific group, in either their speaking, or their writing, or both. University essays are written in the academic register. A writer may develop a specific style or register and sometimes this is known as the writer's *voice*. For nearly all novels the writer needs to be sure they maintain the same register throughout; they don't write *purple prose* and then sparse and spare action. The language of newspaper reporting and that of the popular novel is the register with the clearest, simplest writing.

Dialogue: Dialogue is not reported conversation. Only the essential dialogue of what might be a longer conversation needs to be written. To suggest the speech patterns and vocal mannerisms and vocabulary of a character the writer only needs to use one or two indicators to effectively convey their accents and mode of address. There's no need in dialogue for a lot of half spoken words or uncompleted sentences to suggest authenticity or what a character is thinking. The dialogue can be complete sentences and the writer can let the reader imagine how the character phrases their speaking and their accent and tone of voice.

Point of view: The use of point of view can be made complex by switching points of view in a novel or by having an unreliable narrator, but for popular fiction a clear and consistent choice of using either first or third person point of view throughout a whole book will work well.

Clear use of point of view makes it easy for the reader to find out who they should identify with, and this is what creates the reader's involvement in the story; the reader lives with the central characters wondering what is going to happen to them: this identification with the central characters is one of the great joys of reading.

Create a style sheet: Probably the best way to bring together all the elements that structure the style of writing of a novel is to write out a style sheet. This is a common practice for magazines and newspapers, but can usefully applied to creative writing.

Before the major writing of the novel begins the author will note point of view, use of vocabulary, and specific details such as the use of names, who will be favored in the narrative in terms of inner thought and how the readers are meant to understand the story. On a long piece of writing a style sheet may well prove to be an invaluable guide.

Bad writing: The most commonly encountered problems with fiction writing are that the author presumes that a 'literary quality' is the key to good writing and they write in an over-complex, prolix prose, with an arcane vocabulary, and in doing so they become vague about the story and characters. This happens because a writer thinks that complexity will make a story more intriguing and intelligent. Telling a story clearly and concisely is the challenge for the storyteller. The theory and history of the novel is often taught through eighteenth century classics where a heavily mannered style is appropriate to their setting and period. The classic novel offers good writing, but it is a register of a particular type of novel, class of characters, and from the pen of a writer from a particular period.

Rewriting is essential for excellence: A first draft novel can have a lot of great material in it, but there will be passages that are too long, events in the story that need clarifying and things that can be improved for clarity. Rewriting will structure and focus any novel.

Don't be too precious with first drafts: When an author creates characters and a story this achievement makes the writing precious, and often, new authors feel that nothing can or should be changed with a story because this will damage their ideas. However, by leaving the novel on the shelf for a few weeks after finishing the first draft, then reading it with fresh eyes, the writer will immediately see the weaknesses of a first draft and the need for re-writing becomes clear.

The aim is to tell an involving, entertaining story: An author shouldn't get lost in describing trivia; things that seem interesting, but are tangential to the main events and the central theme of the story. In a first draft, if the writer hasn't prepared a treatment of the story they may well pack in whatever appeals to them. If everything imagined by the writer is included in the final version of a novel it will have a lot of material that isn't essential to the story, which will make it drift and seem unclear to the reader. The writer needs to focus on writing the most important scenes in the story and to summarize the remainder.

Know what the characters want, what motivates them: If the writer has adequately defined their characters during the planning for the novel then it is easy to write for them. The author can set out the goals and motivations for each character using a character profile during the planning of the novel and then this profile will dramatically strengthen the vividness of the characters in the story.

Identify what each chapter must to do: A chapter exists in a novel for a particular storytelling purpose. Once that aim is fulfilled the chapter is complete. There's no need to pad out events simply because it is easy to write more dialogue, or because the action can be described in more detail. New authors are often impressed with how much they have written, but they need to be equally impressed with how much they have cut and edited to make the novel clear.

Test your novel by reading it aloud: Reading a novel aloud as it progresses from first draft to second and then on until completion, will allow an author to identify what is working in terms of story, the clarity of the prose and also enable the writer to recognize what is redundant, unclear, and therefore it needs to be changed. When people sight-read they skim, but when they read aloud they speak every word, and this level of details means that mistakes in grammar and lack of clarity in expression become clear.

Spelling and Grammar; UK and US English: There are differences in vocabulary and spelling when writing in 'English', with two main types. UK English and US English. There is also 'International English', which is, for all intents and purposes, is US English.

A writer should be sure that their book only uses one type of English. This is where a good proofreader will look for errors, and this is an important issue because publishers will not accept a book that is written with a mix of UK and US spelling and punctuation.

One main difference between the two options is that UK English uses 'single quotes' for quotations and direct speech and US English uses "double quotes" for quotations and direct speech.

The best way to ensure that a specific version of English is followed is to study and use a reference guide. As examples of this on-line:

> http://correctpunctuation.co.uk/
> http://englishtoolbox.net/punctuation.htm

Your writing method

When writing, should you check spellings, hone punctuation, re-write sentences, edit and perfect what you have to say as you go? In a short piece of work this may well be feasible. A short essay, or an article, can be corrected as you go and then given a final check and re-check before it's finished, and then it is ready for publication. This is workable because the timescale for the task may be a couple of days, and in this case, checking and re-writing as you progress does not greatly distort the writing process. The same may not be true of a longer work, a full-length novel, where it is better to write a complete draft of the whole book before embarking on any serious process of re-writing, editing or proofreading.

The reason for suggesting this approach, avoiding detailed corrections until you finish, is that until a first draft is complete the main body of novel is not in place and this overall structure may need to be changed.

With a rough first draft, if you want to remove, or add, or combine chapters this can be easily done. However, the time and effort to get to this point will be far greater if each sentence, paragraph and chapter has been carefully worked on. Cutting and revising a whole book after it has been re-written, edited and corrected is a drain, and lot of effort will have been wasted, spending time on correcting details that now need to be cut out completely or extensively revised.

Planning and Writing Your Novel

There are several useful documents that can help you plan a successful novel. They take time to prepare, but they will also save you a great deal of overall effort, in comparison to needing to re-plan, re-write and re-draft an entire novel. They also ensure that a novel will be finished to a high standard; well written, and with a good story. These documents are:

> Story Outline
> Treatment with Chapter Breakdown
> Style Sheet
> Character Profiles
> Sample chapter
> Schedule

Story Outline
If you have an idea for a book, it's good to get this down on paper, so that it becomes a realized idea – something that tangible, and not just a set of thoughts. An outline, one thousand words, can be written in two or three hours and tell a complete story. This can tell you if the plot is viable and complete or if it needs further work.

Outlines are good to store ideas. You might be busy on other work when you get an idea, or not have the time to develop the idea into a full treatment. A story outline is a good basis on which to build and develop the planning for a full novel.

Treatment with Chapter Breakdown
A short version of a novel can be written in 2,000 to 5,000 words. It can set out the story and characters in terms of events and provide a sense of the chapter structure for the book. Most important of all it will be a complete story.

New writers often start a book, but don't finish it, because the story loses momentum. The treatment solves this potential problem by providing an ending. Also, it only takes a few sessions to re-write a treatment and therefore to re-imagine the whole story. To re-work a section of a treatment might involve changing a thousand words while re-writing a book might easily involve changing ten thousand or even twenty thousand words. It's better to work on the story in treatment form.

A treatment will be written as a clear recounting of events. It can be written in the first or third person as suits the viewpoint of the intended book. One might consider the writing of a short story as a type of treatment. Some short stories contain enough plotting to expand into a full novel.

The qualities you are looking for in writing a treatment:

Storytelling: The ability to maintain clarity of action and plot in terms of story and back story. The ability to establish, develop and resolve themes that are set up and developed by the story. The ability to convey a complete and original narrative with a clear (even if complex) dramatic structure, which establishes, develops and closes a narrative with climatic events.

Character: The ability to clearly define, develop and realize the characters in the story: to make the characters credible and consistent in terms of their actions and inter-relationships.

Treatment Example: The following is the start of a treatment for a novel titled; *The Village Boys*. This example makes it clear that a treatment can tell a story in synopsis form which can then be the foundation for a long work of fiction.

The treatment begins with a very brief introduction to each of the main characters, and the plot for the novel is a wartime story aimed at young teenage readers.

After writing this treatment the next stage would be to indicate what the chapter structure will be, although this can be gauged by the treatment. At the moment the double asterix signs ** indicate likely chapter breaks.

The Village Boys
A war-time story

Setting: The coastal village of Porto Levante, North West Italy, Spring 1945.

Main Characters: Three childhood friends, ten years old. They've become wily and independent having to survive the Nazi occupation.

Guy: Proud, overly-brave. He expects to be the leader of the trio.

Jean-Carlo: Intelligent, resourceful. Jean-Carlo could be the leader, but he follows Guy rather than starting a fight for leadership.

Aldo: A follower, somewhat timid, but he wants to be part of the gang.

Treatment

The fierce bright sunshine is gleaming off the Mediterranean Sea as Guy, Jean-Carlo and Aldo are fishing. They are having no luck: it is too hot, the fish are too deep, but they have to get something to eat. The three boys are scrawny and thin. They need a plan to get food.

With a ferocious roar a pair of P-51 Mustangs, American fighter aircraft, flying close to the water, streak by, heading across the wide bay.

Along the coast a road is cut into the rocky hillside. A convoy of lorries carrying troops and equipment is trundling slowly along. It is dangerously exposed.

Heavy caliber shells from the two swooping Mustangs splinter and decimate the vehicles. When the planes have finished using their guns they each drop a bomb on the stranded convoy.

Watching from the distant shore the three boys can see the results of the attack. It does not disturb or elate them; they have seen a lot of bombing. But when the two planes fly back past them they know what they have to do. The three friends quickly reel up their fishing lines and store them in a canvas shoulder bag that Jean-Carlo carries.

**

In the hot dusty village of Port Levante, the small garrison of occupying soldiers' hurry to their open-bed lorry. They are going to help the injured and wounded at the attacked convoy. Once the men are on their vehicle the garrison commander, Dietrich Jaegerman, joins the driver at the front and the troops move away.

Guy, Jean-Carlo and Aldo watch the lorry leave. Then they sneak round to see who's been left to guard the garrison building, which is surrounded by a high barbed wire fence. However, they are too late. Some other village children are already trying to distract the single guard into stepping away from the entrance to the barracks. The two children are coming close, asking for a handout - forcing the guard to shoo them away.

As the guard steps further and further forward, two other, surreptitious children, a boy and a girl, try to sneak behind the distracted soldier. It seems like a game until the guard spots the two children edging behind him, then without hesitating the soldier raises his rifle to his shoulder and he orders them away. It is clear that he is willing to shoot. The children freeze, and then run away.

**

On the coastal road the soldiers from the garrison arrive. Dietrich gives orders. The injured men will be put onto the two lorries in the convoy which are still drivable after the attack from the American fighter aircraft. The uninjured troops will be sent on; continuing their journey on foot. The dead will stay at the roadside, beside the wrecked vehicles, until arrangements are made for new lorries, coming from Genoa, to arrive and take the bodies away. Soldiers from the garrison will stand guard until then.

**

Having lost the opportunity to steal food at the garrison, Guy, Jean-Carlo and Aldo stop at Jean-Carlo's home, a small house in the village. Here, they collect a large jug of water, a big wrought-iron enameled cooking pot, an empty tin can, and a strong long-bladed kitchen knife.

Heading out of town on the main road and stopping at the edge of an olive grove at the bottom of a steep hill the three boys separate into a line: standing well apart from each other they begin.

Each boy walks, taking tiny half-paces, keeping his eyes fixed on the tips of his toes. Guy edges past a crater caused by the explosion of a mine. Next to the crater there is the desiccated corpse of a goat - just the front half.

Aldo calls out: he's found a mine. He carefully marks its position with an olive stick. Then, each boy dutifully back tracks on his path into the grove, and when they are safely in the road, they bicker over who will dig out the mine. Aldo lays claim to the task, because he has found it, but Guy takes the knife and starts back.

**

Taking Aldo's previous path, walking slowly, but with some confidence, Guy gets to the marker stick and checks that it is safe to kneel. He outlines the position of the mine by poking into the ground with the long-bladed knife and then he uses it to lift the crust of hard earth off the top of the glass mine. Breaking the marker stick into four pieces Guy carefully pushes the pieces under the glass pressure plate. When he feels sure that the mine will not go off Guy gingerly digs it out and holding it very cautiously he carries the mine back to the road.

Summary: Treatment with Chapter Breakdown

From the excerpt above it's possible to see how useful a treatment can be. In only five or six thousand words a writer can set out their entire novel in a form where it possible to judge character and plot and also develop a chapter structure for the entire book.

A treatment, in terms of writing will take only four or five days to do, so it represents a relatively small investment in time and effort. The alternative, starting a book with no real plan, or just a vague plot outline, seems like a weak alternative to a treatment; especially when a weak plan can end up wasting days, weeks, even months of time, because a book has to be restarted or extensively re-worked.

Some writers like to develop their story by discussing plot ideas with friends or colleagues. This is a process that can be creative and helpful, but having a treatment is a very clear and certain method for setting out and planning a novel.

Style Sheet

As a useful document for planning a novel the style sheet is taken from journalism where a newspaper or magazine needs to be consistent in its use of language and style, because its articles are written by a wide range of disparate journalists.

For an individual author, and for an individual book, the style sheet provides a guide enabling the author to be consistent for the duration of a long project. The style sheet can deal with any facet of the book that the author feels it is necessary to pin down and define, but it will, more than likely, include the following:

Viewpoint: When will first person be used and when will third person be used? What nuances are there within the use of viewpoint: will it change? How will the use of viewpoint work within the chapter structure of the novel?

Sentences and paragraphs: What style of novel are you writing? Are you writing in the concise contemporary style, using simple sentences with only one or two clauses, or do you have a specific style to match a period story or some other idea? Do you have a single novel, or some other source that provides the model for the types of sentence and paragraphs that your book will use? Will your sentence style be conversational and idiomatic, or will the tone be impersonal and formal?

Vocabulary: Are you matching the vocabulary of your book to a specific period of time, or a particular social group? Here, a list of words and phrases is good. For instance, for a novel set in a legal environment what words are specific to that setting and what idioms or metaphors might be useful to compile. Also, just as important as what vocabulary you might include in the novel, what words might you want to avoid? In a period novel about the English upper classes one might well want to avoid over-familiar clichéd phrases, or conversely, if the novel is a comic parody one might, instead, foreground and overuse every cliché.

Dialogue: How will the dialogue be written technically? Will you use colons or just full stops before dialogue? Will it name the characters after their speech or not? Will the style of dialogue be: 'Hurry up,' Jack said urgently, *or just* 'Hurry up.'

In relation to dialogue it can also be the case that different characters speak in different ways with different vocabularies. This will be outlined in their character profiles, but can be noted in the style sheet to be sure that these differences are emphasized in the actual writing.

Punctuation and grammar: While there are general rules for punctuating sentences are there specific rules for your book? Will it use italics at any point and for what reason? Will it use dashes within sentences? If you've decided to write simple sentences, in the contemporary style, then the need to break up any long multi-clause sentences becomes clear; a more ornate style will need to be carefully defined.

Use of names: In a novel the names of a character are used in two ways. Firstly, how the characters in the novel address each other, and the style sheet should identify the name used during dialogue, noting any use of abbreviations, or alternative names that come into play. Secondly, there is also the use of names of characters in descriptive passages and commentary. In this circumstance will first names or last names be used?

Raymond Chandler for his character Philip Marlowe uses 'Marlowe', while Hammett's character Sam Spade can be identified as either 'Sam Spade' or 'Spade'. Both authors avoid using their central character's first name. The correct use is: 'Marlowe pulled out a gun', it's never 'Philip pulled out a gun.'

The style sheet should also list the correct spellings of character names, to be sure these are used accurately throughout the book. It's 'Philip Marlowe', not 'Phillip Marlow'.

Other things: There may be things that the author recognizes which are vital to keep the story consistent, and they can use the style sheet to itemize these. For instance: for a book set in 1960's the author will want to make sure that only the technology which matches that particular era is used – no mobile phones, no color TV. Other items of interest for this time period would be how much things will cost, like food and petrol.

There are many details that will affect the novel, such as the time of year the book is set in and how does this reflect in the weather and what people wear? Are characters speaking different languages – how will this be handled?

A style sheet helps an author to carefully define their book before it is written, and this can make the writing faster and much better. A book that changes style haphazardly, or gets its story confused, or ends up with an inconsistent plot, will need a great deal of correction and re-working before it is ready for publication.

Style Sheet example

Below is an example of a style sheet. It is for a novel written in the first person, following a single character throughout. It is a contemporary story with a realistic setting. However, viewpoint is carefully controlled in order to create certain narrative effects.

A Visit to My Father
Style Sheet

The story of *A Visit to My Father* is written from the first person point of view of a narrator who the reader will presume to be in their late teens, or early twenties. There is a certain naiveté in the boy's telling of his story, his rather childish descriptions, his simplistic morality, and this is essential to the style of the book.

The reader should sometimes, perhaps quite often, feel that they understand the narrator from a more informed and mature position. This looking down by the reader on the narrator is part of the seduction of the novel. At times the reader will feel that they have a clear judgmental distance from the narrator. However, when the reader is pulled in by the story and they accept its directness as real and honest, this will make their identification intense and complete, because they will feel that they have always been able to extract the truth of the story.

The book is a narrative novel. The style matches the storyteller. None of the writing or plot should be perceived as experimenting, or exploring literary devices or style. The writing is pragmatic, not literary. The writing uses the common register. The story is clearly and directly expressed. Any undue literary description or phrasing is inappropriate. There is some use of colloquial phrases where they support the realism of the writing, but these should not be overused. The story is not written in the vernacular.

On a few occasions the narrator directly addresses the reader. This is to give the reader a little persuasive 'kick': it makes it clear that the writer knows that the reader is there and that the author is telling the reader the story. Talking to the reader directly is an openness on behalf of the writer/narrator, and is intended to make the reader more complicit in the story because they know that 'the writer of this story is talking directly to me'.

Characters and names: The narrator tells the story at an emotional distance. The narrator of the story is never named and remains always in the first person.

The father in the story is always 'my father.' He is never just 'father' and certainly never 'dad', or 'daddy'. This absolutely strict device is because of the dominance and absolute authority that 'my father' carries. The character of the father is fixed and immutable.

The mother is referred to both as 'my mother' and 'mother'. There is no set rule for which option is used, and this choice is dependent on the tone and meaning of the specific sentence and paragraph.

As a general guide when the narrator is mentioned in the sentence as 'I', or 'me', the possessive 'my' mother is used. This rule can also be applied to a paragraph when the narrator is clearly writing about 'my mother'. The use of just 'mother' is most suitable when the narrator is describing events in which he is not directly involved.

The highly controlled use of an unnamed narrator, with parents who are never given proper names, entirely suits the characters, and their relationships.

Chronology: The story spans events covering twenty years and for contemporary terminology to drift into descriptions of another era would be a weakness. Anachronisms are to be avoided, especially in dialogue. The events are usually told as they are happening, not as remembrances, and for the purpose of stylistic coherence the same register is kept throughout the book. While it's clear that the story happens in different eras, all reference to books, or films, or products, or brands, that define the era are avoided. The central character is not defined by being a consumer.

Setting: The book names specific towns and streets to create a sense of place and reality, but it is a work of fiction. Any events taken from real life have been transposed and synthesized into a fictional world. However, given that the book is set in real places, with recognizable settings, these must appear accurate.

The story is set in Britain, it is a British story, and therefore American spelling, phrasing, or terminology is to be avoided.

Punctuation: There are several aspects of punctuation and layout that need to be carefully checked and confirmed:

- Sometimes the use of commas has been based on the stresses that a person reading the book out loud would use. The book should be punctuated correctly according to grammatical rules.

- Ensure the correct use of a colon at the end of paragraph before dialogue when this identifies who is speaking.

- Remove unnoticed use of US spellings or phrases

- Remove the repetition of a word in the same sentence or paragraph when there is a suitable synonym.

- All speeches use single apostrophes in the English tradition. i.e. 'I am speaking.'

- There is no use of exclamation marks in dialogue. This is because there are so many speeches that might suit its use that it would appear overdone.

- A few speeches use capitals. This is only done where there is a specifically strong emphasis on the speaker's tone, or volume.

- There is no use of italics to stress words in a speech, or other words

- The first line of a chapter is not indented. All other paragraphs are indented.

- It is has been the fashion in many recent books to use single sentences as entire paragraphs for dramatic effect. This is a device whose novelty is waning and it should be avoided in new books. It appears now as a mannered manipulation of the reader and may even weaken good writing that needs no such treatment.

Summary: Style Sheet

There is no set format for the style sheet. It defines and confirms how the novel is written, so the author can include whatever achieves this aim.

The example above, which is an extract from a style sheet, shows how clear and specific this sort of document can be, and how it will then be very helpful to the author. Beginning a book without knowing how it will be written is a very uncertain process, and the lack of competence in the writing can easily lead to a new writer producing a book that is not written to a professional standard; stylistically it will be uneven, and it will be inconsistent in terms of setting, character, and plot.

Character Profiles

Everyone has seen a film or read a book and gone; 'that character wouldn't have done that.' This is the moment that the character's behavior is not consistent and the story loses credibility.

For the characters in a novel to appear realistic they have to behave in ways that are consistent with their established character. The writer needs to know who the characters are, where they're from, what the characters believe; their personalities. How a character will act in any situation has to have a sense of purpose and unity and if this fails then the whole story is in trouble. This is one of the reasons why writing a character profile, setting out what motivates and underpins each character is important.

The other reasons for writing character profiles is to be sure that characters are consistent in terms of how they look, move and speak during the course of a book. When a novel can take more than a year to write it's easy to forget exactly what a character is meant to look like and changes and errors can creep into the text.

The character profile also sets up the relationships between characters and also their back stories and this depth of history and relationships gives the characters a sense of life outside of the confines of the book. It can also help an author to use the same characters in another novel.

It's not uncommon for writers to use the same character again and again; sometimes with major characters in one novel, becoming minor characters in another novel. Characters exist in their own right and have their own personal histories and stories. For a character profile it's good to decide on the followings details:

The social background and cultural identity of the character: These are the specific details of the character; name, age, race etc., and these are factors that put a person in a particular social and historical context. They will also influence how a person speaks, dresses, gestures, and also their beliefs and knowledge. All these characteristics represent a person's social identity. One might say that these are the externally discernible aspects of character, because they might be noted down on a census form. They don't tell you very much about an individual personality.

The character's personality: This would include their super-objective; what they want from life. While personality is to some extent flexible; a person is unlikely to be an entirely *kind person*, they are more likely to be kind in some circumstances, but not in others. However, it is still useful to create a sense of how a character is likely to behave and react in a range of situations.

Personality sets out a number of motivations. For example a character in a story who likes company might seek out a friend and then they might be more willing to put up with bad behavior from that friend which others might condemn. Such a situation might create a conflict that could be the basis for a story. Personality is also about emotion. Is the character usually tense, happy, angry; what mood does this person convey as a personality?

The abilities of the character: What can they do, and also, just as importantly, can't do. This will strongly influence their behavior in a range of situations. This might also include their abilities due to their intelligence.

The character's sense of themselves: A character may have a sense of themselves that is in tune with their personality and social identity, or they may be confused or mistaken about who they are. For example someone who is selfish may think of themselves as taken advantage of, or a miserly person may think of themselves as very poor and in need of money. A mismatch between ability, personality and a person's conscious understanding of themselves can contribute to a drama by creating an ongoing conflict. You can see this aspect of character emphasized in comedy, where for example, a person who thinks he is charming and funny is actually a braggart and a bully. Comedy is often about people's ideas about themselves not being sustainable, or not standing up to scrutiny from others.

The relationship between the characters creates changes: People's actions, reactions, decisions and thoughts are, more often than not, highly dependent on their relationship with others; It matters a great deal who someone is loyal to, who they hate, who hates them, and this will strongly dictate what someone will do. Dramatic circumstances occur when a range of characters meet up; there will be alliances and antagonisms, that will develop and change during the course of a story.

To develop a character profile it might be good to use the headings set out below and write a sentence or two about the character under each of the headings below:

Personal Attributes	**Social background**	**Individual Characteristics**
Name	Social status	Behavior
Appearance	Cultural identity	Emotional characteristics
Accent	Social history	Moral characteristics
Speaking style	Race	External motives
	Ethnicity	Hidden motives
	Family history	Subconscious motives
Abilities	Job	Ruling passion
Dress	Friends	Defining relationships
	Money	Defining Beliefs
		Self-image
		External image

Sample chapter

If you're clear what style your book is going to be written in, this is good, and it can be confirmed by writing a sample chapter, or even just a part of a chapter. This will demonstrate what the book is going to look like when it's written and this sample provides a template for the whole novel.

Obviously, in many cases, an author will have various ideas about what might be the correct style for a particular book, and each of these different options can be considered more concretely by writing sample pages: a first person version, a third person version, a colloquial style, an omniscient style. It's easy to try out different styles by writing short passages. It's a lot of work to re-write a whole book if you become dissatisfied with the style of writing at a later stage.

Other Planning and Research Material
The story outline, treatment, style sheet, and other documents that help you plan your novel, can be supplemented by a wide range of planning and research material. In fact, by anything you find useful to help create and imagine the story. These could be photographs, maps, drawings, diagrams, films, books, even objects. You can also create specific materials to support your creativity: J.K Rowling drew pictures of Hagrid, so she could imagine this over-sized giant. J. R. R. Tolkien drew maps of the kingdoms where his characters lived.

Diagrams can be used for plotting, or for timelines, or for noting character attributes and appearance. Some writers prefer diagrams, or the use of index cards for plotting, and these can be used instead of writing a treatment in prose. There are a number of computer programs that support novel writing, and whatever the writer uses for planning or research the purpose is to imagine the story world, the characters and the plot, before beginning a full first draft of the book.

A schedule to write and complete your novel
Your writing history, what type of writing you've done, how often and how much you write, gives you some idea of your proficiency as a writer. Can you write a thousand words at a sitting or three hundred? Do you write regularly, so that you know you have the stamina for a long piece of work? Can you control the style of writing in order to be able to write quickly? Will you need to take breaks from writing in order to re-plan and re-think your novel? All of these will influence how long it takes to write a long work, but to create a simple schedule for a novel the following two formulas can be used:

Length of planned book
÷
Average word count for a writing session
=
The number of sessions to write the first draft of the novel

As an example :

$$\frac{80,000 \text{ words for the book}}{500 \text{ words per session}} = 160 \text{ sessions to write the first draft of the novel}$$

This is the second useful formula:

$$\frac{\text{The number of sessions to write the first draft}}{\text{How many writing sessions each week}} = \text{The number of weeks to write the first draft}$$

As an example:

$$\frac{(80,000 \text{ word book}) \; 160 \text{ Sessions}}{4 \text{ sessions per week}} = 40 \text{ weeks to complete the first draft.}$$

Working with these calculations, an 80,000 word book, which is structured, with somewhere between thirty and forty chapters, means that the estimated schedule results in the author writing roughly a chapter a week in order to complete the novel. This is quite a demanding output. The work of re-writing, editing and proofreading a novel is likely to take half as long as the first draft, so the time for writing the novel from start to finish, using the schedule above, will be roughly eighteen months. For a part-time writer this would be a fast pace of work and something to be very satisfied with.

The contemporary style for popular fiction allows for fast concise writing, but literary fiction will take far longer to draft and a full-time literary novelist is unlikely to produce a book in less than two years. If a book is very long and very complex the writing can take a very long time: Joseph Heller worked on *Catch-22*, part-time, for ten years (it was worth the effort) and three to four years is a common length between starting and finishing a novel for a literary writer.

Some people like schedules and deadlines and some people don't. If you don't want to set a schedule with a deadline marked on the calendar then it is probably still a good idea to keep track of the progress of your writing. This might be a week-by-week total, or a month-by-month word count of how the novel is progressing. Using this system you're not setting a specific time-based deadline, but you are tracking your progress to see if the work is going well or the work is going slowly. Just a note in a diary or on a calendar will indicate what's been written over a particular period of time. If the output slows, then the effort needs to be made to pick up the pace.

Writing Your Novel

This is a model for writing a novel to a professional standard in an efficient and productive way:

Developing the story and the story structure

You can write out the story of your novel as a short treatment and get a first opinion from people you respect as readers or as writing professionals. They should share your tastes and understand what genre and style of literature you are trying to write.

If an author finds that everyone who reads a treatment seems confused and unclear, then the plot needs work. When everyone expresses doubts and suggests that the central character will be universally despised then this character may need re-thinking. If no one mentions a section of the story and shows no interest in it then this part of the narrative may be unnecessary; it can be cut from the story or minimized so that it takes up less time to tell.

When taking advice on a treatment or idea, the aim is not to change your story to match every comment, but to gather comments in order to see how your story is coming through; how others perceive it.

The experience of storytelling is by definition is a two-part process; writer and reader, storyteller and listener, and the writer can benefit from getting a sense of how the reader will understand the story by testing their ideas at the development stage. Writing a whole novel and then finding out that nobody understands it, or enjoys it as you intended, is not a good idea.

To get useful and supportive advice find people you can trust to get feedback from, don't ask the opinions of people who have little or no interest in reading fiction novels, because they may well reply without thinking about their responses.

Testing sample chapters of your book

Once you begin writing the first draft of your novel it's a good idea to make sure that you've chosen the right style for your book. Don't ask someone to read several chapters, or half a book, because you're not asking about the story, (you did this when you discussed the treatment) but have them read a sample chapter. Ask them to offer suggestions about editing, changing sentences, the use of vocabulary, the effectiveness of the dialogue.

What you want feedback on is writing technique and at this stage you can even do things like change the style of the book or change point of view, if that then seems like the best thing to do. For this type of feedback you need to ask someone who knows how to write; an experienced writer or a publishing professional. This is a person who can compare your work to a professional standard. Making the effort to get this sort of advice can save a great deal of editing and re-writing later, because it will focus the writing style, and when you're confident about what you are doing you will be able to write faster and to a higher standard; all of which is good.

Once you have taken an opinion on both the story and the writing style then it's probably time to get down to writing and finishing the whole first draft.

First draft

After planning your novel with a treatment, and a breakdown of the chapter structure, write the book swiftly. Keep moving forward. If some sentences aren't as well expressed as they should be this can wait, if there is obvious over-writing let this stand. If you hit a problem and don't quite know how to write an event in the story then make a note of what you need to write, what part of the story is missing, and then just jump over this section and return to write it later. During a first draft don't get stalled because you get stuck on a small issue, such as how to describe a house, or what a character is wearing.

When you have finished the first draft consider the whole book. Is the story what you want? Are the characters developed? Is the action coherent and credible? If you need to cut drastically, to add new elements, or even re-structure the whole novel, this is the time do it. Edit broadly, cutting and pasting, not getting bogged down in details.

When you are more experienced you might establish a daily word count, say five hundred words per day, and you will expect this writing to be completed to a professional publishing standard. It is very good if you can write to this high level of quality in the first draft, but if this goal is set, but not maintained, and your daily plan for a set word count bogs you down; writing sessions end up being about making small corrections, or re-writing a small set of sentences again and again. Then it is better to write with more speed, leaving some errors to wait, because you plan to re-write.

It is only after editing is completed, and you have a second draft of your book, one that needs no major re-editing, that you finally get down to honing each paragraph and sentence.

Re-writing

When the book has a chapter structure that works well, and successfully tells the story, then start re-writing each chapter. Re-writing means working to make sure that expression - what each sentence states in terms of action or description - is as it should be. The aim is to achieve clarity. Material can be added where necessary, as can cutting out what is badly written, confusing, or unnecessary to the story. Bad writing consists of awkward phrasing, convoluted description, and unnecessary, ponderous commentary.

The aim here is not to proofread each word, in terms of perfect spelling and punctuation, but to improve on the first draft, so that any problems of expression or clarity of writing are reduced. For instance, a paragraph that is confusing can either be amended and re-written or cut out and written again from fresh.

Editing

Once a book is re-written and it's in good shape - it's beginning to look like a novel that can be published - then the role of the writer changes. They become an editor. The creative writer is the person imagining, creating, building the narrative structure, and telling the story. The editor is scrutinizing the detail; the choice of vocabulary, the use of punctuation, the breakdown of paragraphs, the control and use of speech. Editing brings the book into line with the style decided for the novel; it's ensuring coherence in terms of the style sheet: ironing out the use of viewpoint, making sure that punctuation and grammar are correctly done.

At this stage the author does not have to be the person doing the work, and, in fact, the author may find this editing difficult to do, because rather than editing they will start re-writing, which is a stage that needs to be finished before this close, final, sentence by sentence editing takes place.

Proofreading

This is technical job; looking for errors and omissions; misspellings, missed punctuation. It's the final stage and takes the book into a form ready and finalized for publication.

The value of clearly dividing the writing process, first draft, re-writing, editing, proofreading, is that at the start of the process the writer doesn't have to worry about EVERYTHING. If on the first page of a novel the writer feels like a sentence is unclear and they stop and re-write and re-write and re-write, then the book becomes an enormous, potentially overwhelming task.

Dividing the writing of a book into separate parts allows the author to concentrate on what is most important. In the first draft it's telling the story, in the re-writes its adding clarity to the story, in editing it's refining the style of the writing, and in proofreading it's ensuring that any typographical errors are corrected.

Support for your writing

There is no reason why writing needs to be a lonely, isolated task. Of course a writer will spend many hours working by themselves, but a book can be developed with the support of others, and certainly, in the later stages of re-writing, editing and proofreading, having knowledgeable advice, having professionals working on a book is an approach that improves the writing.

It's a great support having an editor who can indicate what they think needs to be changed. They can mark up the book; indicating sentences that need work and question parts that could be better written. The editor is like a coach for a sports person: they are an expert who raises the level of the practitioner. As with all advice a knowledgeable professional person is best. Editing is not something for a friend to do; they may be too cautious, they may not have the skills required.

Proofreading is not a task for the writer because when this stage is reached the author will have read the book so many times and gone over so many options that reading the book just for spelling, punctuation and grammar is almost impossible. A proof reader can be given a clear set of guidelines; how names are to be spelt, how sentences and speech are to be punctuated and they can work through the book checking these; having no interest in the story of the book.

The author will read their book after it is proofread so they can indicate where a correction is missed or the wording has been incorrectly changed. However, the book should then go back to the proofreader. The author should not embark on their own proofreading process because they are likely to start re-writing and changing, just to correct or alter a lot of work that might be sorted out with the insertion or removal of a few commas or a semi-colon.

It's hard for the author to work on their book and to be completely content with how it's written, but once proofreading is done then the book is complete; if it's not good enough to publish then, the next book will be. A writer has to reach a point when they accept that the book is finished. The writer will dislike, or be uncertain about some of the things in the book, but the re-writing and re-working of the same book can't go on forever.

Publication and Reviews

When a book goes to publication the writer is very happy but also very uneasy. Having a finished book is great, but there are always going to be dissatisfactions; passages the author doesn't like, choices they are unsure about.

What it is good to be aware of is that when a book is reviewed, the critics have their own agenda; they can compare one book to any other book that takes their fancy, and they can create any criteria they feel like for criticizing a book.

A critic may take umbrage that a book is set and tells it story in Genoa, because they think the story would work better if it were instead set in Pisa. This sort of random-thinking criticism happens because the job of the reviewer is to take an angle on a book so they have something to say to fill up the words in a review. Book reviewers aren't so much interested in the novel itself, and they are reviewing it more for what they have to say, and in terms of what they think the book should be like: they don't care about the intentions and the feelings of the author.

When a writer gets an infuriating, negative review, and this criticism makes the whole book seem pointless, this is hard. But, here it's important for an author to remember that there's a strong tendency for critics to feel they are better critics if they are more critical, and often critics set a standard for the perfect book; a novel without fault which is written with exactly the story and in the style that the critic wants to read. In fact, this perfect book is something that doesn't exist, and the critic is just using this spurious idea of literary perfection in order to make comments on a published work.

One thing that critics are not really concerned with is the process of writing. If a writer wants an opinion on their writing ability they should ask someone who is engaged and committed to their work; a genuine reader. Those who have read the book to experience the story will have comments and questions that are pertinent and are to be valued. Above all else the writer has to take their own counsel; they worked on the book, they know it, they can judge it and criticize. And from this understanding of their work the author can improve their writing in future work. Even if a book is praised to the skies by a reviewer a shrewd writer will treat this with great caution because the writer knows their book better than anyone else: they know it's not perfect.

Post-publication reviews and criticism is not to be confused with advice and support during the writing of the book. When a book is finished what a writer needs to be more concerned with than anything else is their next book. The next book is where the challenge and satisfaction is. What happens after publication is not within the writer's remit.

What's best for an author is to receive knowledgeable advice during the writing of their book and to concentrate on this to guide the style and quality of their future writing. Nearly all successful authors will be the subject of some dreadful reviews and adverse criticism; this is not advice to follow; it is not intended to help the writer.

Writing a Book for Publication

Commercial publishers want to publish books by writers who have the potential to be a committed author with a long-term career. For a writer to be commercially viable they have to have a readership and they can do this by writing novels within a genre that is popular, or that appeals to a particular readership (which has significant numbers), or the author can develop a readership through reputation and critical review.

Your book will be considered for publication if it is: written proficiently in terms of style, story, and in terms of spelling, punctuation and grammar. The submission of a book that is not well written is the simple reason why most manuscripts sent to agents and publishers will not go any further than a first-look, and also, why an author may have to write two or three books before they are published.

Your book will be considered for publication if it has: a central character or characters and a setting that can be developed into a series of books.

A novel that can catch the reader's attention with a compelling central character, and therefore develop an identity in the marketplace, is the key to long-term commercial success. This type of book is what a publisher needs to sustain their business. These are series characters such as Sherlock Holmes, Harry Potter, Robert Langdon, Kay Scarpetta, Miss Marples.

Your book will be considered for publication if it is: written within a popular genre; crime, thriller, romance, suspense or horror. Within genre writing there are books that are rather over-familiar in terms of story, but there is a dedicated readership for these types of stories and if there are several books are in a series then readers will want to know what happens to their favorite character: so they will buy more books from this author. Genre, serial-book writing is the mainstay of commercial fiction publishing.

A book will be considered for publication if it is of particularly high literary or social merit so that it will attract critical support through book reviews and award nominations. Publishers do not expect to sell large numbers of a literary work, but hope for a breakthrough book that establishes a new literary author, which makes them commercially viable.

So, in terms of publishing what type of author will you be?

> I'm writing in an established genre, with a compelling central character, that I plan to use in several books. *This is a strong, professional and commercial approach.*

> I'm writing a literary work that I hope will garner nominations, prizes and positive critical reviews. *A singular work is less likely to be published, and it is competing for publication and readership against all other established literary authors. This kind of author needs to have long-term aspirations. To be a novelist whose work and merit will eventually become established, and this status and recognition will, in turn, support a commercially viable level of book sales.*

> I'm writing a story that is a one-off and very specific to my own interest and tastes. I don't plan to write many books. *This is the kind of book and approach to writing that is least likely to appeal to publishers: even when, on its own merits, the novel is well written and well told. This book hasn't been written for a wide readership and the author does not plan to develop a long-term career that will develop a substantial readership.*

It's fine to write a commercially minded book, especially if you enjoy the joys of the genre and enjoy your setting and central characters. It's also fine to write for literary merit, because of the appeal and enjoyment of literary writing, and it's fine to write a book simply because the subject appeals to you, and to your own personal taste and interest. However, being clear about what type of book you are writing gives you a realistic expectation regarding it chances for commercial publication, and crucially what your aims need to be if you want to be a commercially successful writer. Any book that looks like a memoir, or a thinly veiled autobiography, looks to a publisher like a one-off book and publication is unlikely.

If you are determined to write for commercially successful publication then it's necessary to work to the demands of the book industry and they want authors who plan for long careers writing popular fiction.

What's good about the situation today is that if you don't want to write a commercially driven novel in order to support a full-time professional writing career then you can self-publish and distribute a book yourself, and this can be far more satisfying than being rejected by a long list of publishers, or ending up with a book that doesn't sell more than a few copies because it receives no reviews and bookshops don't want to stock it.

If your book has a specialist readership, perhaps because of its setting or subject, you can use the web to promote your book to a reader who will want to read your work. In this case self-publishing may be better than commercial publishing, because the author controls their own book, and crucially, its marketing. Commercial realities mean that publishers will always support their most successful and established authors.

It's hard for a new writer to get a high level of support for publicity and marketing which then translates into book sales. Each new writer has to generate a readership that competes with a publisher's already popular authors. Often, good, even excellent books, written by unknown authors, can simply disappear in relation to the promotion of famous authors and their eagerly anticipated bestseller.

As a creative writer you can develop lots of ideas, for many different types of stories, and this means that if you feel that your first book must have the best chance of publishing success, you can develop and write a story that suits this option. What you can't do is simply write a novel to your own personal taste and then expect a publisher to support it: publishers need writers who can develop a readership, and this is a commercial criteria that an author must bear in mind before deciding which book they are going to write.

Final word

The aim of this book has been to help you understand what creative writing is, how to develop your storytelling skills; how to define yourself as a writer, how to develop your storytelling technique and how to plan, schedule and successfully complete your first novel.

The work of writing your novel needs to be done, you need to make the time to write, to put in the effort needed for good writing, but you can use what this book has offered you, and use it to achieve your ambition to be a writer.

Most of all, enjoy your writing, and when you publish your first book, please let me know, or even send me a copy.

Referenced Authors
Alphabetical by first name

Alexander Dumas
Bernard Cornwell
Bernhard Schlink
Brett Easton Ellis
Carl Hiaasen
Charlaine Harris
Charles Dickens
Colin Dexter
Dan Brown
Dashiell Hammett
Donna Tartt
Edith Wharton
Ernest Hemmingway
F. Scott Fitzgerald
Fyodor Dostoyevsky
George Bernard Shaw
George Orwell
Gustave Flaubert
Guy de Maupassant
Henry James
Hunter S. Thompson
Ian Fleming
J. R. R. Tolkien
J.K Rowling
Jack Kerouac
Jane Austen
John Grisham

John Sandford
John Steinbeck
Joseph Conrad
Joseph Heller
Joyce Carol Oates
Kathy Reichs
Lee Child
Leo Tolstoy
Maya Angelou
Michael Connelly
Molière
Natsuo Karino
Norman Mailer
Oscar Wilde
Patricia Cornwall
Patricia Highsmith
Raymond Chandler
Roald Dahl
Robert Harris
Sarah Waters
Stephanie Meyer
Thomas Harris
Tom Clancy
Virginia Woolf
William Burroughs
William Goldman
Yukio Mishima

Referenced Books

Affinity
Angels and Demons
Anna Karenina
Black Sunday
Catch-22
Chasing the Dime
Fingersmith
Grotesque
On the Road
Our Lady of The Flowers
Out
Real Girls
Red Dragon
The Count of Monte Christo
The Da Vinci Code
The Grapes of Wrath
The Great Gatsby
The Narrows
The Outsider
The Piano Teacher
The Reader
The Rules of Attraction
The Secret History
The Way Through The Woods

INDEX

A, B and C Storylines, 53
Archetypal, 78
Back Story, 68
Bad Writing, 109, 129
Beats, 76
Chapter Breakdown, 13, 47, 48, 49
Chapter Structure, 13, 53, 60, 113, 129
Character Beat, 77
Character Profiles, 14, 113, 122
Characters and Names, 120
Clarity and Simplicity, 105
Classic Literature, 91
Climax, 11, 25, 51, 71, 96, 100
Comic Writing, 81
Commentary, 41, 67, 92, 9, 118, 129
Complications, 55, 69
Defining Yourself as a Writer, 37
Developing the Story, 127
Dialogue, 100, 108, 118
Disruption of Equilibrium, 67
Editing, 13, 129, 130
Establish, 18, 43, 68, 95, 106, 128
Feedback, 46, 48, 127, 128
First Person, 54, 60, 94, 95, 119
Foreshadowing, 11, 68
Genre, 20, 21, 78, 102, 132, 133
Hero, 20, 21, 55, 72, 79, 80, 97
Idioms, 106
Immediate Action, 89, 107
Inciting Incident, 67
Inspiration, 17, 19, 43
Internal Thoughts, 60, 95
Jig-Sawing, 11, 17, 19, 35, 43, 65
Journalism, 40
Length of Planned Book, 125
Misdirection, 70
Mythic Storytelling, 78
Narrative Beat, 77
Narrative Terminology, 8, 11, 14
Non-Fiction, 10, 37, 40, 47
Pay off, 68

Planning and Writing Your Novel, 113
Point of View, 67, 108
Popular Fiction, 89, 103
Proofreading, 129, 130
Publishing, 9, 15, 46, 128
Punctuation and Grammar, 105, 118
Raising the Stakes, 71
Realism, 78, 80, 93, 120
Register, 108
Relationships, 75
Research, 10, 14, 19, 26, 37, 59
Reversals, 69
Re-Writing, 13, 129
Roman à Clef, 22, 26, 43
Sample Chapter, 113, 124
Scene Objective, 74
Schedule, 42, 59, 125
Sentences and Paragraphs, 92
Set Up, 68
Stereotypes, 72
Story Outline, 13
Story World Conventions, 66
Storytelling Terminology, 11, 37, 78
Structuring your Novel, 49
Style Sheet, 14, 113, 117, 122
Summary Action, 89, 90, 107
Super-Objective, 73, 124
Surprise, 70
Suspense, 70
Temporality, 89, 99, 100, 105
Tension, 54, 76
Terminology for Storytelling, 65
Third person, 53, 60, 95, 113
Three-Act Dramatic Structure, 49
Treatment with Chapter Breakdown, 13, 113, 117
Turnarounds, 69
Unseen Action, 71
Use of Names, 118
Viewpoint, 20, 27, 37, 53, 60, 61, 62, 6 91, 113
Vocabulary, 93, 107, 117
Writing Session, 12, 15, 125
Writing Technique, 89

Eugene Doyen writes novel for young adult and teenage readers:

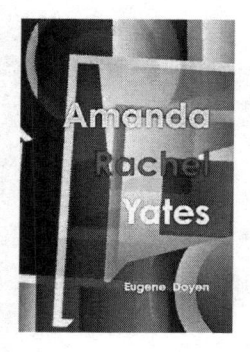

Amanda Rachel Yates

Amanda wants to help her mum, but everything is falling apart. Rachel, Amanda's mum, is out of control. She's taking too many pills, drinking too much, and shoplifting, rather than spending money on food. Amanda is trying to cope. Then Rachel gets into a fight with a teacher and Amanda goes into care. Will Amanda fight to stay with her mum, or let herself be moved to a foster family?

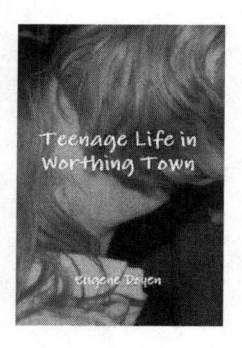

Teenage Life in Worthing Town

In Worthing, a seaside town in West Sussex, there's an under-eighteen disco each Wednesday night in the pier ballroom. It's naff, but it's the only place where boys can go to meet girls, and where girls can go to meet boys. It's the best chance they've got to meet someone they want. This is *Teenage Life in Worthing Town*.

The Family History

There's no sense talking about what a family should be. You might say that a mother should love her child, and a father should love his son, but that's all from the outside. Inside, there is only the family. There's no love, there's no forgiveness. There's only what happened. This is what I know and this is what I have to tell you: the family history.